Dear Family Member,

Many children think that math = difficulty. Scholastic's *100 Math Activities [?]
Grade* will help your third grader realize that understanding + practice = [?]

Children need practice in order to develop mathematical thinking an[d?]
need engaging examples in order to make abstract math ideas concrete. [?]
opportunities in order to work successfully with math concepts and symbols. Your third gr[ader?]
find all of that in our colorful, educational, *fun* activities.

The 100 activities in this workbook will help your child build his or her understanding of and
facility with the key concepts and operations involved in

- number sense
- place value
- addition and subtraction
- multiplication and division
- fractions

- measurement
- geometry
- time
- money
- organizing data

A Math Skills list, on page 224, highlights the math skills in all of the activities in this workbook.
These essential skills relate to the math curricula and standardized tests your child will be exposed
to in school.

We've included a sheet of reusable math stickers, which your child can use to create number or
word equations, solve number problems, and engage in all kinds of creative math play.

You are an important part of your child's math education, so we've also provided a few
suggestions below for easily integrating math into your daily routine.

Scholastic's *100 Math Activities Kids Need to Do by 3rd Grade* will give your child math
competence . . . and confidence. Enjoy!

Jean Feiwel
Scholastic Publisher, Senior Vice President

Parent Tips

- Make sure your third grader knows what to do on every activity page. When he or she
  solves a problem, ask, "How do you know?" The more reasoning your child gives, the better.
- Put the math stickers where your child can easily see and reach them. Challenge your child
  to solve a new sticker equation each day.
    - Play math games while you're driving, preparing meals, waiting in
      line, sitting in waiting rooms. They might include
        - saying two multidigit numbers and asking which one is greater
          than or less than the other
        - saying a four-digit number and asking which numeral is in the
          ones, tens, hundreds, or thousands place
        - saying a number such as 12 and asking your child for its factors
          (1, 2, 3, 4, 6, 12) or its multiples (12, 24, 36, 48, . . .)
        - playing "I spy" based on geometric shapes
    - Use fractions and measurements while cooking with your child: "Give
      everyone one-fourth of the pizza." "Add 1 cup of milk." Or play a
      fractions game: "Which would you rather have, one-third of this pie or
      two-eighths of it?"
    - While grocery shopping, ask your child to compare products by size
      or price. Pick an item and ask what coin/bill combinations would
      add up to its price. Put several items in a cart, and ask your child to
      round off each price and add up the total.
    - Help your child make a graph showing the daily weather for a
      month.

Editor: Sheila Keenan

Art Director: Nancy Sabato

Managing Editor: Karyn Browne

Production Editor: Bonnie Cutler

Project Management: Kevin Callahan, BNGO Books

Composition: Kevin Callahan, Patty Harris, Tony Lee, Daryl Richardson

Copyeditor/Proofreader: Geraldine Albert, Abigail Winograd

Cover: Red Herring Design

Editorial Consultant: Dale A. Beltzner, Jr., Elementary Math Specialist, Lower Milford Elementary School, Coopersburg, Pennsylvania

Activity Pages Writer: Jackie Glasthal

Activity Pages Illustrator: Beegee Tolpa

Contents

Math the "Write" Way

There's only one way to spell out the numbers 1 to 10 in this puzzle grid. Can you find it? Hint: Once you know where the **one** goes, the rest should be as easy as 1-2-3!

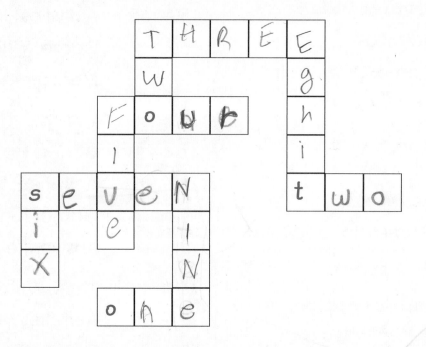

Now follow these directions to find out how you can turn any number into a **four**.

1. First, pick any number. 17

2. Spell it. *seventeen*

3. Count the number of letters in the word. 9

4. Spell that number name. nine How many letters in it? 4!
   Keep repeating steps 2 and 3. No matter what number you start with, you'll soon end up with **4**!

Go 4 it! Use the instructions on page 4
to turn each of these numbers into a 4.

Your age

1. _9___

2. _____

3. _____

4. _____

4 letters!

Number of brothers and sisters you have:

1. _____

2. _____

3. _____

4. _____

4 letters!

Your street address:

1. _____

2. _____

3. _____

4. _____

4 letters!

Number of rooms in your home:

1. _____

2. _____

3. _____

4. _____

4 letters!

What's the first number that when spelled out
contains the letter **a**?

_____

Hot Diggity Numbers!

Spell the names of each of these numbers.

24 $\bigcirc$ _ _ _ _ _ - _ _ _ _ _

18 _ _ _ _ $\bigcirc$ _ _ $\bigcirc$ _ _ _

31 _ _ _ _ $\bigcirc$ _ _ - $\bigcirc$ _ _

11 _ $\bigcirc$ _ _ _ _ _

12 _ _ $\bigcirc$ _ _

62 $\bigcirc$ _ _ _ _ - $\bigcirc$ _ _

83 $\bigcirc$ _ _ _ _ - $\bigcirc$ _ $\bigcirc$ _

101 _ $\bigcirc$ _ _ _ _ $\bigcirc$ _ _ _

HOLLYDOG

208 ◯___ ___ ___ ___ ___ ___ ___ ___ ___ ___

___ ___ ◯___ ___ ___

2,000 ___ ___ ◯___ ___ ◯___ ___ ___ ___ ___ ◯___

892 ◯___ ___ ___ ___ ___ ◯___ ___ ___ ___ ___

___ ___ ___ ___ ___ - ___ ___ ◯___

418 ___ ___ ◯___ ___ ___ ___ ___ ___

___ ___ ◯◯___ ___ ___ ___

Write the letters you circled above in order to answer the riddle below.

Why didn't the hot dog want to star in the movies?

___ ___ ___

___ ___ ___ ___ ___

___ ___ ___ ___ ___ ___

___ ___ ___

___ ___ ___ ___ ___

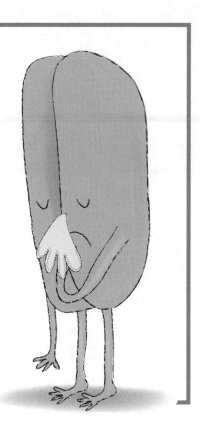

Picturing Place Value

What's the difference between the numbers 22 and 2? The number 22 has 2 more groups of 10 in it than the number 2.

Write how many more groups of 10 one number has in it than the other.

_____ more group of 10

16   6

_____ more group of 10

20   10

_____ more groups of 10

30   10

_____ more groups of 10   4

24

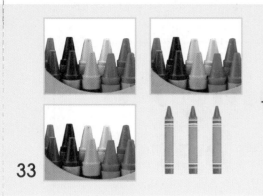

33 _____ more group of 10

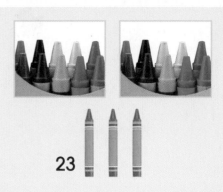

23 _____ more groups of 10

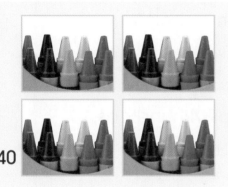

40 _____ more groups of 10

10

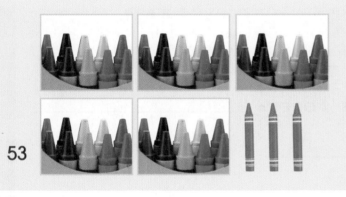

53 _____ more groups of 10

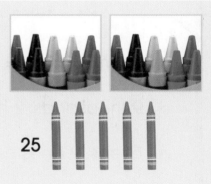

25

100 _____ more groups of 10

10

Calling All Numbers!

Place value helps you write numbers in a short form.

Example:

8 thousands, 4 hundreds, and 6 ones = 8,406

Rewrite each number below in short form, as a numeral.

a. 8 tens, 7 ones = _____

e. 9 thousands, 2 hundreds, 6 tens, 4 ones = _____

n. 5 tens, 9 ones = _____

f. 2 hundreds, 6 tens, 1 one = _____

w. 1 thousand, 8 hundreds, 6 ones = _____

b. 2 thousands, 4 tens = _____

i. 3 tens and 2 ones = _____

d. 1 ten thousands, 5 tens, 5 ones = _____

l. 4 hundreds, 5 tens, 4 ones = _____

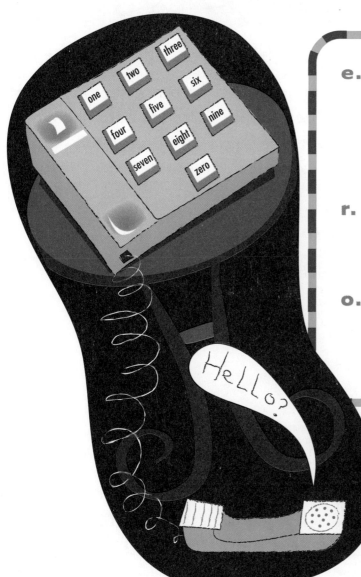

e. 1 thousand, 8 hundreds, 6 tens, 6 ones = 1,866

_____

r. 2 thousands, 4 ones =

_____2,4008_____

o. 9 hundreds, 8 tens, 1 one =

_____9,81_____

Order the numbers on these pages from least to greatest.
The letters next to the numbers will spell out the answer to this riddle.

Where does Mother Nature take her naps?

___ ___   ___

___ ___ ___ ___ ___ ___   ___ ___ ___

Places, Everyone!

The human body is an amazing machine! Use the place-value clues to learn more about it. Read the facts and the clues. Write the correct numbers from the box.

Remember:

millions	hundred thousands	ten thousands	thousands	hundreds	tens	ones
1,	0	0	0,	0	0	0

23	750	103,689
23,040	104	62,000
4,800	32,000,000	25,000

Most humans produce about _____ quarts of spit in a lifetime. That's enough to fill two swimming pools!
Place-value clue: There's a 5 in the thousands place.

You move about _____ muscles each day.
Place-value clue: There's a 5 in the tens place.

You speak about _____ words every day.

Place-value clue: There's an 8 in the hundreds place.

Air from a sneeze can travel at _____ miles an hour.

Place-value clue: There's a 4 in the ones place.

There are _____ miles of blood vessels in every human body.

Place-value clue: There's a 2 in the thousands place.

Every square inch of your body has about _____ bacteria living on it. (But don't worry—many of these are the good bacteria that help you to digest food and protect you from illness.)

Place-value clue: There's a 2 in the millions place.

In one day, your heart beats about _____ times.

Place-value clue: There's a 1 in the hundred thousands place.

You take about _____ breaths daily.

Place-value clue: There's a 4 in the tens place.

It takes your blood about _____ seconds to make a complete trip through your body.

Place-value clue: There's a 2 in the tens place.

Round 'Em Up

Help! These horses have gotten loose! Draw a line from the rounded number on each saddle to the corral that the horse belongs in.

To figure out what place value a number has been rounded to, look at the first digit from the right that is not a zero. Figure out that digit's place value. That's your answer!

Examples

230 is rounded to the nearest ten.

5,000 is rounded to the nearest thousand.

Hold That Place!

Standard notation form is the way we usually see numbers written out. For example, **6,302**.

Expanded notation form lets you see the value of each digit within a number. For example, **6,000 + 300 + 2**.

To complete this puzzle, change each number from **expanded notation form** to **standard notation**. Don't forget to use zeroes as placeholders wherever they belong!

Across

A. 200 + 20 + 1

C. 600 + 90 + 7

E. 50 + 7

G. 400 + 80

H. 30 + 7

J. 2,000 + 300 + 80 + 4

L. 2,000 + 100

N. 10 + 5

P. 900 + 80 + 2

Q. 20 + 1

S. 500 + 5

T. 100 + 40 + 4

Down

A. 2,000 + 800 + 40 + 3

B. 100 + 80 + 5

D. 90,000 + 800 + 40 + 1

F. 700 + 20

G. 40 + 8

I. 70,000 + 2,000 + 800

K. 300 + 2

M. 10 + 2

O. 5,000 + 400 + 90 + 4

R. 100 + 10 + 1

Place-Value Machine

An abacus is a counting machine invented in ancient China. It is still used in some countries today. On an abacus, each row of beads stands for a different place value.

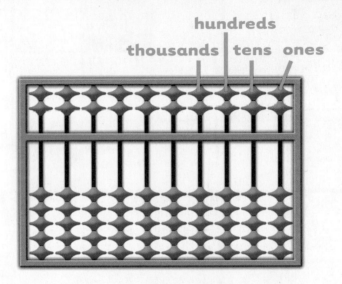

thousands hundreds tens ones

The beads at the top of the abacus stand for **5** units.
The beads at the bottom each stand for **1** unit.
To show a number, move the beads toward the center.

Examples

The abacus above shows 0 (no beads are toward the center).

This abacus shows 7.

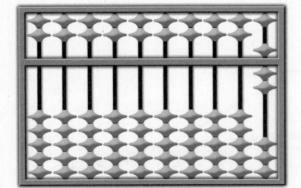

This abacus shows 8,742.

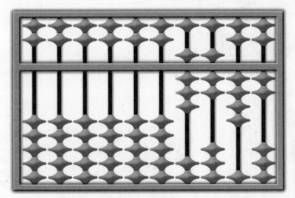

Write the number shown on each of these abacuses.

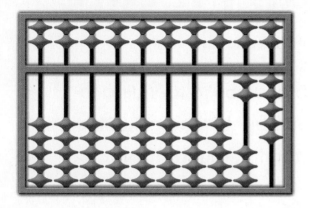

_____

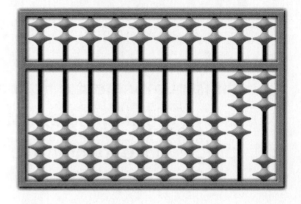

_____

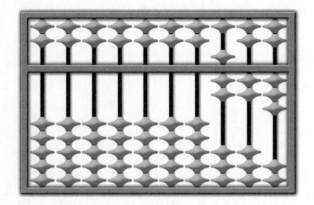

_____

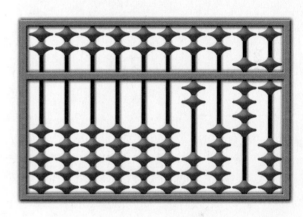

_____

Draw an abacus showing a two-digit number.	Draw an abacus showing a five-digit number.

A Place-Value Picture

Find out who's hiding in this place-value picture by rounding off.

If the number to the right of the place you're rounding to is **5 or greater**, round **up**. If the number to the right of the place you're rounding to is **less than 5**, round **down**.

Round these numbers to the nearest **ten**.

52 _____   229 _____   1,063 _____   63 _____

16 _____   176 _____   28 _____   74 _____

134 _____   91 _____   107 _____   78 _____

8 _____

8,000

4,000

900

2,400

70

130

2,000

10,000

10

80

3,000

50

7,000

400

20

100

13,000

1,000

Round these numbers to the nearest **hundred**.

311 _____   1,129 _____   445 _____

98 _____   879 _____   2,439 _____

Round these numbers to the nearest **thousand**.

897 _____   6,121 _____   9,499 _____

4,259 _____   7,400 _____   9,768 _____

2,222 _____   11,299 _____   12,455 _____

8,145 _____   2,989 _____   12,700 _____

4,726 _____

Color in numbers rounded to the nearest ten **green**.

Color in numbers rounded to the nearest hundred **brown**.

Color in numbers rounded to the nearest thousand **blue**.

11,000

300

230   30

60

180

110   1,060   9,000

90   5,000

1,100   12,000

6,000

Palindrome Puzzlers

Palindromes are words or numbers that read the same backward and forward. The words **mom**, **pop**, and **pup** are palindromes. So are numbers like **77**, **101**, and **24,233,242**.

Read the clues, and write the palindrome numbers they describe. The first one has been done for you.

I am a two-digit palindrome number with an 8 in my ones place. __88__

I am a four-digit palindrome number with a 1 in my thousands place and a 5 in my hundreds place. _____

I am a palindrome number between 500 and 510. _____

I am an odd-number palindrome that is greater than 11 and less than 50. _____

I am a four-digit palindrome number greater than 9,000 with a 6 in my tens place. _____

I am the greatest possible five-digit palindrome number. _____

I am the greatest possible palindrome number between 200 and 300. _____

I am the least possible palindrome number between 800 and 900. _____

Now come up with your own number–palindrome riddle, and share it with a friend!

_____

_____

_____

_____

Reading Between the Numbers

> **>** means greater than
>
> **<** means less than
>
> **≥** means greater than or equal to
>
> **≤** means less than or equal to

Write the numbers that fit each number set.
The symbols in the box will help you.

> 25 but < 37 =

____ ____ ____ ____ ____ ____ ____

____ ____ ____

> 49 but < 65 =

____ ____ ____ ____ ____ ____

____ ____ ____ ____

< 212 but > 202 =

_____ _____ _____ _____ _____

_____ _____ _____ _____

≤ 79 but ≥ 68 =

_____ _____ _____ _____ _____ _____ _____

_____ _____ _____

≥ 84 but ≤ 98 =

_____ _____ _____ _____ _____ _____ _____

_____ _____ _____ _____ _____ _____

Now, write the missing numbers, based on the numbers shown.

> _____ but < _____ = 2,000, 2,001, 2,002, 2,003, 2004

> _____ but < _____ = 150, 151, 152, 153, 154, 155, 156

< _____ but > _____ = 1,031, 1,030, 1,029, 1,028, 1,027,
1,026, 1,025, 1,024, 1,023, 1,022,
1,021, 1,020, 1,019

≤ _____ but ≥ _____ = 10, 9, 8, 7, 6, 5, 4, 3, 2, 1, 0

≥ _____ but ≤ _____ = 56, 57, 58, 59, 60, 61, 62, 63, 64, 65,
66, 67, 68, 69, 70

Dizzy Digits

What happens when you rearrange the digits in the number 15? Suddenly you have 51! In this game, the goal is to use the digits you spin to create the greatest number you can!

You Need

- players
- the spinner on this page
- a paper clip
- pencil and paper

Use the pencil and paper clip to make an "arrow" for the spinner. Flick the paper clip. It will spin around the pencil point.

1. Each player draws five lines on a sheet of paper. Write the place value — **ten thousands, thousands, hundreds, tens, ones** — under each line.

2. Take turns. Spin the spinner. Write the number you spin on one of the five lines that you drew. Remember: The goal is to create the largest number you can.

3. When each player has filled in all five lines, the player who has created the highest number wins that round.

4. The first player to win five rounds wins the game.

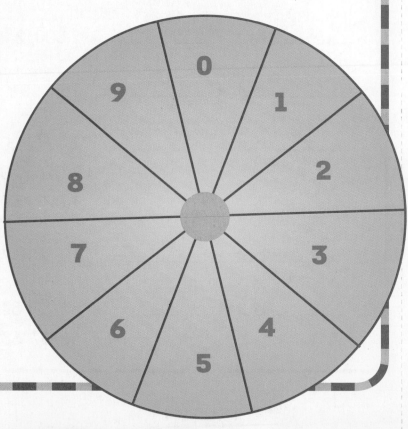

Number Sense & Place Value Answer Key

Note: Answers read across, per page.

4–5 See below; answers will vary but should work out to 4; one thousand

6–7 twenty-four, eighteen, thirty-one, eleven, twelve, sixty-two, eighty-three, one hundred one, two hundred eight, two thousand, eight hundred ninety-two, four hundred eighteen; the rolls were not good enough

8–9 1, 1, 2, 2, 1, 3, 3, 9

10–11 87, 9,264, 59, 261, 1,806, 2,040, 32, 10,055, 454, 1,866, 2,004, 981; in a flower bed

12–13 25,000, 750, 4,800, 104, 62,000, 32,000,000, 103,689, 23,040, 23

14–15 Tens: 20, 250, 320; Hundreds: 300, 2,800, 3,200, 9,800; Thousands: 4,000, 23,000, 28,000

16–17 See below.

18–19 25, 53, 723, 2,096; answers will vary.

20–21 Ten: 50, 230, 1,060, 60, 20, 180, 30, 70, 130, 90, 110, 80, 10; Hundred: 300, 1,100, 400, 100, 900, 2,400; Thousand: 1,000, 6,000, 9,000, 4,000, 7,000, 10,000, 2,000, 11,000, 12,000, 8,000, 3,000, 13,000, 5,000

22–23 1,551, 505, 33, 9,669, 99,999, 292, 808; answers will vary.

24–25 26, 27, 28, 29, 30, 31, 32, 33, 34, 35, 36; 50, 51, 52, 53, 54, 55, 56, 57, 58, 59, 60, 61, 62, 63, 64; 211, 210, 209, 208, 207, 206, 205, 204, 203; 79, 78, 77, 76, 75, 74, 73, 72, 71, 70, 69, 68; 84, 85, 86, 87, 88, 89, 90, 91, 92, 93, 94, 95, 96, 97, 98; 1,999, 2,005; 149, 157; 1, 032, 1,018; 10, 0; 56, 70

4–5

16–17

Find That Number

Write in the numbers described in the clues. Then add or subtract.

Goldilocks and the _____ Bears —

number of ears you have _____ = _____

Number of noses you have _____ +

number of horns on a unicorn _____ = _____

A _____ -leaf clover —

New Year's Day is January _____ = _____

Number of kids in a set of twins _____ +

number of players in a game of checkers _____ = _____

One, _____ , buckle my shoe +

_____ , four, shut the door = _____

Wheels on a bicycle _____ +

wheels on an automobile _____ = _____

Fingers on one hand _____ +

eyes on one face _____ = _____

Legs on an octopus _____ +

number of real unicorns _____ = _____

Snow White and the _____ Dwarfs +

number of things in a pair _____ = _____

Sides on a cube _____ +

sides on a square _____ = _____

Find the pattern formed by the sums or differences in these equations.
Then write your own "Find That Number" equation, using
the answer that should come next.

_____ = _____

Target 10

Can you count by tens? Fill in the missing numbers in each series.

10 20 30 _____ 50 60 _____ _____ 90 100

110 _____ 130 140 _____

4 14 24 34 _____

54 64 _____ 84

94 104 _____ 124

_____ 144 154

22 32 42 _____

_____ 72 _____

92 102 112

_____ 132

Now add 10 to each of these numbers in your head; then write your answer.

90 _____

410 _____

650 _____

770 _____

775 _____

Using patterns of 10, find the sum of each equation.

50 + 30 = _____   111 + 50 = _____

90 + 10 = _____   615 + 60 = _____

42 + 20 = _____   832 + 30 = _____

21 + 40 = _____   1,425 + 50 = _____

79 + 40 = _____   3,214 + 60 = _____

Be a Nine Reader!

To be a nine reader, you must be able to add 9 to a number without using a pencil. Look at these nine readers, and see if you can find a pattern to their solutions.

There are two patterns.

$$9 + 3$$
___
$$12$$

The ones column in the sum is 1 less than the number in the ones column you were adding to 9.

$$10 + 3$$
___
$$13 - 1 =$$

Add 10, and then subtract 1.

$$9 + 3$$
___
$$12$$

Use the above strategies to help you solve these math equations.

$$9 + 7$$
___
16 s

$$9 + 14$$
___
23 o

$$66 + 9$$
___
75 c

$$9 + 39$$
___
48 y

$$52 + 9$$
___
61 e

81
+ 9
90 u

108
+ 9
117 n

98
+ 9
107 a

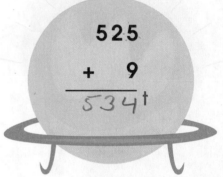

525
+ 9
534 t

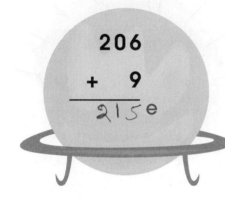

206
+ 9
215 e

Now use the letters next to your answers to solve the riddle below.

What did the fortune-teller say when an invisible man asked to have his fortune told?

Sorry, I

____ ____ ____ , ____
75   107   117   534

____ ____ ____   ____ ____ ____
16   215   61   48   23   90

right now.

Math March

Add each set of numbers in your head.
Look for groups of easy numbers to help you.

8 + 17 + 2 = _____r

60 + 7 = _____p

95 + 5 + 12 = _____e

30 + 15 = _____a

$7 + 16 + 3 =$ _____ n

$32 + 8 + 40 =$ _____ l

$5 + 23 + 55 + 10 =$ _____ h

$25 + 25 + 10 =$ _____ e

$9 + 110 + 21 =$ _____ a

Now use the letters next to your answers to solve this riddle.

What is a rabbit's favorite kind of transportation?

A ___ ___ ___ ___ - ___ ___ ___ ___ ___
  93   140   27   60   67   80   45   26   112

Math States

Add the numbers below. Draw lines to match the sums to the numbers next to the names of the states. You've just located that town! Look in the box if you need help regrouping when you add.

Remember:

1. Add the ones column. (Think: 9 + 5 = 14)

$$\begin{array}{r} 59 \\ + 95 \\ \hline \end{array}$$

2. Regroup, and record the 14 like this:

$$\begin{array}{r} {}^{1}59 \\ + 95 \\ \hline 4 \end{array}$$

3. Add the tens column. Don't forget that the 1 really stands for one ten (14 = 1 ten + 4 ones), so it is added to the 50 + 90 already in the tens column.

$$\begin{array}{r} {}^{1}59 \\ + 95 \\ \hline 154 \end{array}$$

1. Bee Lick

$$\begin{array}{r} 14 \\ + 7 \\ \hline \end{array}$$

2. Burnt Corn

$$\begin{array}{r} 19 \\ + 19 \\ \hline \end{array}$$

3. Embarass

$$\begin{array}{r} 15 \\ + 17 \\ \hline \end{array}$$

4. Fleatown

$$\begin{array}{r} 22 \\ + 69 \\ \hline \end{array}$$

5. Gnaw Bone

```
   58
+  32
_____
```

6. Hungry Horse

```
   69
+  13
_____
```

7. Peculiar

```
   98
+  22
_____
```

8. Worms

```
   86
+  15
_____
```

170	South Carolina
32	Wisconsin
120	Missouri
91	Ohio
82	Montana
38	Alabama
121	West Virginia
101	Nebraska
21	Kentucky
90	Indiana

9. Ninety Six

```
   73
+  97
_____
```

10. Odd

```
   82
+  39
_____
```

On Track with Addition

Add. Write the sums.

$$
\begin{array}{r} 314 \\ + 12 \\ \hline \end{array}
\qquad
\begin{array}{r} 912 \\ + 55 \\ \hline \end{array}
\qquad
\begin{array}{r} 419 \\ + 12 \\ \hline \end{array}
$$

$$
\begin{array}{r} 670 \\ + 88 \\ \hline \end{array}
\qquad
\begin{array}{r} 732 \\ + 89 \\ \hline \end{array}
\qquad
\begin{array}{r} 624 \\ + 82 \\ \hline \end{array}
$$

918
+ 99

76
+ 216

37
+ 118

47
+ 891

78
+ 702

378
+ 90

How many sums have a 7 in the hundreds place? _____

How many sums have 4 digits? _____

How many sums are even numbers? _____

How many sums are odd numbers? _____

How many sums have a 2 in the tens place? _____

How many sums have a 6 or an 8 in the ones place? _____

Awe-Sum!

Add. Watch your tens, hundreds, and thousands places!

486 + 143	812 + 35	16 + 14	41 + 50	309 + 363

38 + 25	40,000 + 7,883	36,405 + 36,405	1,001 + 1,163	1,536 + 1,709

94,600 + 1,872	42,251 + 44,241	19 + 49	88 + 423	16 + 13

```
  11,403        526          14           54          718
+ 32,183      + 217        +  9         + 36        + 134
---------     -------      -------      -------     -------


     29         380       20,018         998        4,800
  +  19       +  99     + 78,228     + 17,180     + 1,446
  -------     -------   ----------   ----------   ---------


  18,070        156         550          877          416
+ 20,479      + 206       + 178         + 38        + 117
---------     -------     -------      -------     -------
```

Go Number Fishing!

The big fish are the sums. Which two smaller fish add up to those amounts?
Write your five equations below. Hint: You can use each number only once.

_____ + _____ = _____

_____ + _____ = _____

_____ + _____ = _____

_____ + _____ = _____

_____ + _____ = _____

Lucky Signs

These two rabbits forgot where they dug their burrow.
Can you help them get back to their hidden rabbit hole?
Use these signs:

> means greater than
< means less than
= means equal to

Find the signs that point the rabbits down the
path with only true number equations.

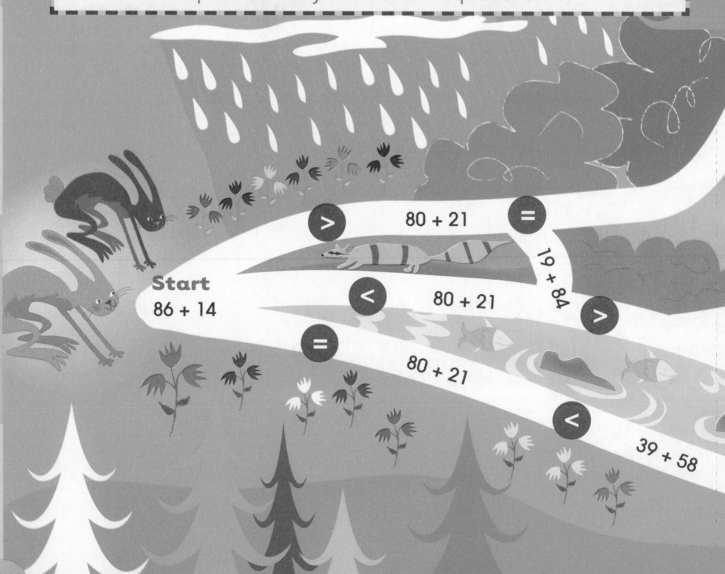

Start
86 + 14

> 80 + 21 =

19 + 84

< 80 + 21 >

= 80 + 21

< 39 + 58

Subtraction

Subtract. Find the differences.
Regroup if you need to.

Remember to regroup.

1. If you can't subtract the ones column, regroup from the tens column first. (Think: 1 ten + 4 ones = 14). Now you can subtract 9 from 14.

$$\begin{array}{r} 1\overset{4}{\cancel{5}}\overset{1}{4} \\ -\ 95 \\ \hline 59 \end{array}$$

2. Subtract the tens column. Regroup from the hundreds column if you need to. Don't forget that you already borrowed from the tens column.

$$\begin{array}{r} \overset{0}{\cancel{1}}\overset{14}{\cancel{5}}\overset{1}{4} \\ -\ 95 \\ \hline 59 \end{array}$$

3. Subtract the hundreds column. If there is a 0 in the hundreds column, you do not need to write it in the difference.

$$\begin{array}{r} \overset{0}{\cancel{1}}\overset{14}{\cancel{5}}\overset{1}{4} \\ -\ 95 \\ \hline 59 \end{array}$$

$$\begin{array}{r} 15 \\ -\ 13 \\ \hline \end{array} \qquad \begin{array}{r} 65 \\ -\ 42 \\ \hline \end{array} \qquad \begin{array}{r} 99 \\ -\ 89 \\ \hline \end{array} \qquad \begin{array}{r} 456 \\ -\ 254 \\ \hline \end{array}$$

40	76	267	538
− 11	− 29	− 189	− 483

18	728	37	965
− 9	− 438	− 18	− 476

How many differences are > 100? _____

How many differences are < 100? _____

How many differences are > 20 but < 60? _____

Breezing Through Subtraction

Draw a kite string to match each subtraction equation with its difference.

$$219 - 6$$

$$478 - 19$$

$$82 - 13$$

Remember:
Subtract numbers in the ones column first. Next, subtract the tens followed by the hundreds. Regroup if you need to.

$$48 - 6$$

$$389 - 95$$

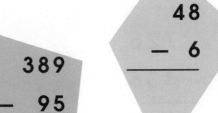

606

42

395

294

$$411 - 16$$

$$558 - 89$$

$$708 - 98$$

$$880 - 416$$

$$712 - 106$$

$$726 - 708$$

$$629 - 114$$

469

464

18

459

515

610

69

213

Inventions with a Difference

When were each of these objects invented? Subtract to find out.
Then write the inventions where they belong on the timeline.

television

6,979
− 5,052
‾‾‾‾‾‾‾

talking doll

4,998
− 3,112
‾‾‾‾‾‾‾

telephone

3,999
− 2,123
‾‾‾‾‾‾‾

the Internet

6,984
− 5,011
‾‾‾‾‾‾‾

1565   1762   1853   1876   1886

sandwich

1,788
−   26
―――――

flashlight

9,998
− 8,100
―――――

pencil

1,797
−   232
―――――

Velcro

7,969
− 6,021
―――――

zipper

2,995
− 1,105
―――――

potato chips

2,964
− 1,111
―――――

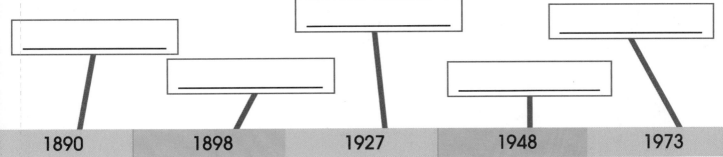

| 1890 | 1898 | 1927 | 1948 | 1973 |

Bone Up on Subtraction

When you were a baby, you had about 350 bones in your body. As you grow, some bones join together. How many bones do most adults have? Solve the subtraction equations to find out.

When subtracting from a number that ends in more than one 0, regroup more than one place at a time.
Example:

$$\begin{array}{r} \overset{9}{\cancel{1},\cancel{2}\cancel{0}\cancel{0}} \\ -\ 1,186 \\ \hline 14 \end{array}$$

hands

$$\begin{array}{r} 2,500 \\ -2,462 \\ \hline \end{array}$$

shoulders

$$\begin{array}{r} 200 \\ -196 \\ \hline \end{array}$$

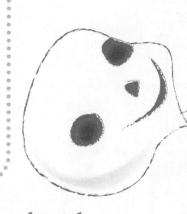

head

$$\begin{array}{r} 100 \\ -\ 71 \\ \hline \end{array}$$

chest

$$\begin{array}{r} 5,000 \\ -4,975 \\ \hline \end{array}$$

wrists

$$\begin{array}{r} 7,000 \\ -6,984 \\ \hline \end{array}$$

arms

$$\begin{array}{r} 1,000 \\ -\ 994 \\ \hline \end{array}$$

legs

75,000
− 74,992
_____

ankles

260,000
− 259,986
_____

hips

10,000
− 9,998
_____

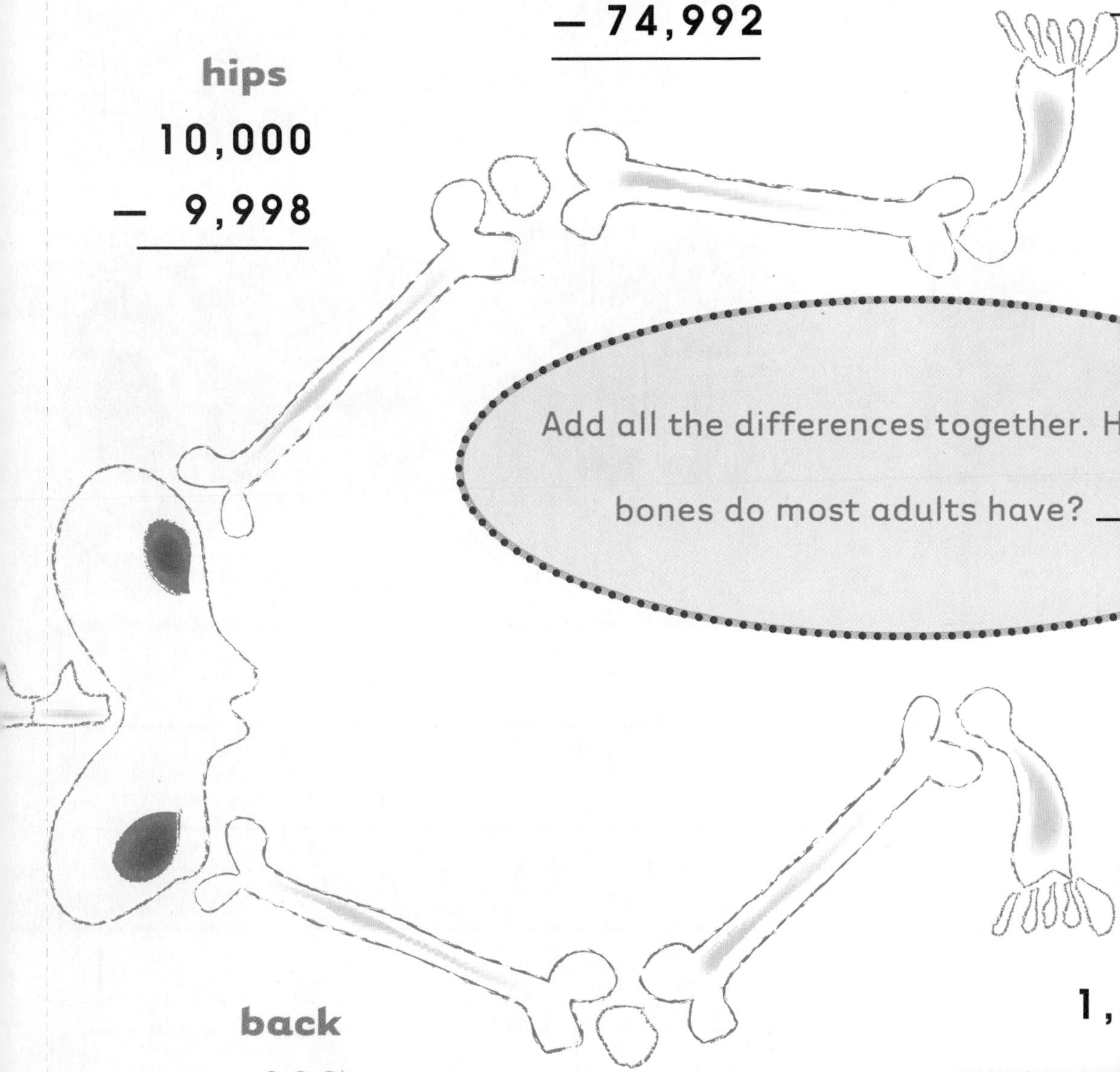

Add all the differences together. How many

bones do most adults have? _____

back

300
− 274
_____

feet

1,000,000
− 999,962
_____

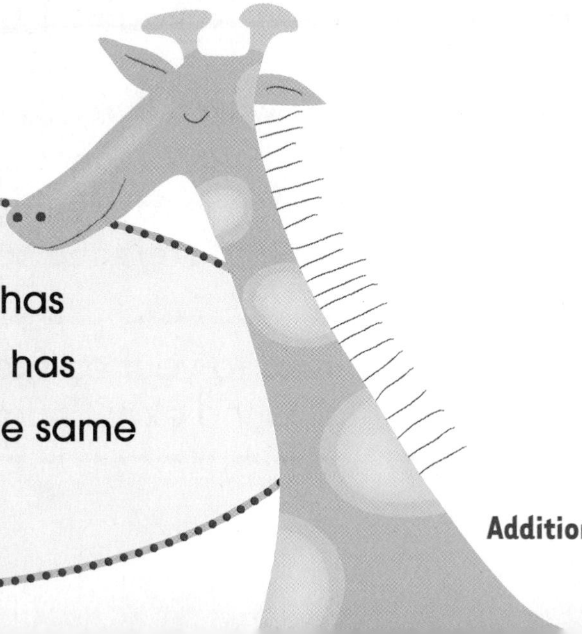

Fun Fact: Even though it has such a long neck, a giraffe has only seven neck bones—the same number as a person!

Estimates and Exact Numbers

How many times could you do each of these activities in one minute? Take your best guess (called an **estimate**), and write it in the "Estimates" column.

Activities	Estimate	Exact Number	Difference
Touch your toes.			
Clap your hands.			
Bounce a ball.			
Write your name.			
Pat your head, and rub your stomach.			

Now test your estimates with a clock or a stopwatch. Write the results in the "Exact Number" column. Subtract. Write the difference between the estimates and exact numbers in the "Difference" column.

> Put a check ✔ next to your estimate that came closest to the exact number.

Here are some examples of when estimates and exact numbers come in handy. Circle the letter next to the situations in which an **estimate** is all you need. Underline the letter next to the situations that require an **exact number**.

Do you need an exact number or an estimate when you

n. solve a subtraction equation on a math test at school

c. pay for an item that you are buying at the store

e. figure out how much wrapping paper you need to wrap a present

s. measure a piece of wood to fit in your bookcase as a shelf

n. add water to a pot in order to cook spaghetti

t. measure out the ingredients needed to bake a cake

i. check today's temperature before deciding what kind of clothes to wear outside

e. take your temperature to find out if you are sick

n. take a count of the number of people who are watching a parade

Now unscramble the letters you circled and the letters you underlined to find the answer to this riddle.

What's the difference between an old penny and a new dime?

_____ _____ _____ _____   _____ _____ _____ _____
(circled letters)   (underlined letters)

What's the Good Word?

Use these clues to help you fill in the missing math words.

When you see the words **is less than**,

you'll probably need to __ __ __ __ __ __ __ __.

When you __ __ __ __ __ the number 38
to the nearest ten, you get 40.

In the number 392, the 9 is in the __ __ __ __ place.

The solution to an addition equation is called the __ __ __.

The answer to a subtraction equation

is called the __ __ __ __ __ __ __ __ __ __.

The symbol = is called an __ __ __ __ __ __ sign.

When an exact number is not needed,

you can use an __ __ __ __ __ __ __ __ instead.

The numbers 2, 4, 6, 8, and 10 are all __ __ __ __ numbers.

The numbers 1, 3, 5, 7, and 9 are all __ __ __ numbers.

In the number 12,420, the 0 appears in the __ __ __ __ place

Circle your word answers in this puzzle. The words can read down, up, backward, and diagonally and may appear more than once.

s l a u q e b s e c e
u u a d s c u e e s s
b e m e d n t v s t t
t h n e y e a e t c i
r o l w a r e n i a m
a t e n s e v d m r a
c y s f v f e s a t t
t s n e t f n u t b e
l t n u f i f m e u q
d n u o r d d o d s f

That's Sum Difference!

Addition and subtraction are **inverse**, or opposite, operations.

That means you can check subtraction equations by adding.

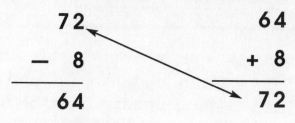

$$72 - 8 = 64$$

$$64 + 8 = 72$$

And you can check addition equations by subtracting.

$$79 + 115 = 194$$

$$194 - 115 = 79$$

Now you try! Use inverse operations to check these equations. If the equation is not true, change the **=** (equals sign) to a **≠** (does not equal sign). Circle the letters next to the remaining true equations.

e 10 + 19 = 29

h 94 — 12 = 82

r 17 — 6 = 12

r 14 + 7 = 23

t 17 + 6 = 23

r 45 — 14 = 44

r 39 + 11 = 51

c 58 + 12 = 70

e 48 + 14 = 62

a 48 + 18 = 66

h 71 — 39 = 32

r 94 — 26 = 69

Unscramble the letters next to the true equations to solve this riddle.

What animal is a sore loser when it comes to sports and games?

A _____ _____ _____ _____ _____ _____ _____!

Soaring with Math

Enter a number (any number!) on the side of the plane.
Then do the math equations along the route. Each time you reach
a cloud, you should be back at your starting number!

Addition & Subtraction

+ 26 _____ − 10 _____ + 19 _____ − 35 =

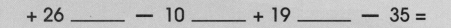

_____

+ 548 _____ − 372 _____ − 124 _____ − 41 _____ − 11 =

_____

+ 59 _____ − 34 _____ + 16 _____ − 41 =

_____

Are We There Yet?

Will Travel and his family have planned a cross-country road trip.
The map shows some of the cities they plan to visit along the way.
Use the map and the distances shown on it to answer these questions.

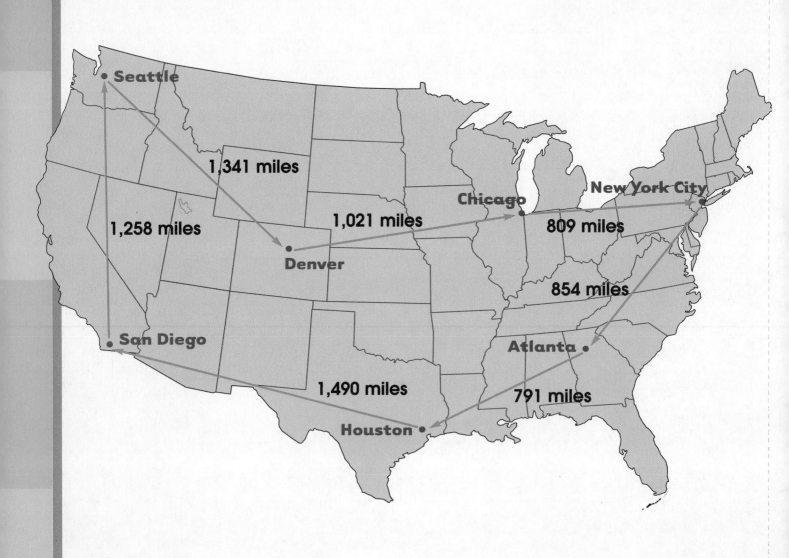

1. Of the cities Will and his family plan to visit, which two are

   farthest apart? _____ and _____

2. What is the distance between these two cities? _____

3. Of the cities Will and his family plan to visit, which two are nearest

   each another? _____ and _____

4. What is the distance between these two cities? _____

5. How many miles total will Will and his family travel between

   Denver and New York? _____

6. How many miles total will Will and his family travel between New

   York and Houston? _____

7. How many more miles will Will and his family travel when they

   drive between Chicago and New York than when they drive

   between Atlanta and Houston? _____

8. How many more miles will Will and his family travel when they

   drive between Houston and San Diego than when they drive

   between San Diego and Seattle? _____

9. What will be the total distance Will and his family will travel on their

   cross-country trip? _____

Mixed-Up Word Problems

Not all math word problems are silly — but these are!
To make them even sillier, write a word on the line as described.
(Don't read the problem first!) Then read and answer each question.

Tanya's Pet-Walking Service

To make some extra cash, Tanya started a pet-walking service. Her first customer, _____ (friend's name), asked Tanya to walk her 8 pet _____ (insects). But then each pet brought 3 friends along. How many pets did Tanya walk in all? _____

Justin the Junior Juggler

When Justin's mom told him that he couldn't take juggling lessons, Justin decided to learn on his own. He juggled

3 _____ (food) on Monday,

4 _____ (noun) on Tuesday, 6

huge _____ (animal) on Wednesday,

8 _____ (noun) on Thursday, and 12

_____ (noun) on Friday before taking a break for the weekend. How many items had Justin juggled in all by the end of the week? _____

Birthday Blues

Brian was bummed. For his birthday, all 20 of his friends gave him the same kind of _____ (clothing).
Of these, 2 were _____ (color), 6 were _____ (color), and 5 were _____ (color). The rest were orange with red, yellow, and purple polka dots. How many of the presents had red, yellow, and purple polka dots? _____

Late Luke's Morning Routine

Every day Late Luke leaves himself 55 minutes

to get ready for school. He takes 15 minutes to eat

his _____. It takes him another 15 minutes to
      food

brush his _____. He uses the rest of the time to
      body part

put on his _____. How much time does Late
      type of clothing

Luke leave for his third morning activity? _____

Carlos's Collections

Of all Carlos's kooky collections, his most treasured is his 983 assorted

_____. It was his favorite, that is, until his friend Erica traded him 423
      toys

of her 720 _____ for 386 things from Carlos's collection. How many
      another toy

of his favorite things did Carlos have left after the trade was made? _____

How many things from her original collection did Erica still have? _____

Peter Piper's Packages

Peter Piper was proud of picking a peck of pickled peppers.

He decided to pick up some other stuff as well. After putting

down the peppers, he lifted 6 packs of _____, 4
      food

bushels of _____, and 8 crates of _____
      food   noun

before falling over and calling a back doctor. How many

packages did Peter Piper pick up after putting down the

pickled peppers? _____

Math Moves Mountains!

What are some of the tallest mountains in the world? Use these facts in an equation to figure out the answers. Write your equations.

Mauna Kea, an inactive volcano on the Big Island of Hawaii, is actually taller than the tallest mountain on earth — if measured from its starting point on the ocean floor, that is. From the ocean floor, Mauna Kea stands 33,476 feet tall. That's 4,448 feet higher than Mount Everest, which is considered the tallest mountain. How tall is Mount Everest?

_____

The fifth highest mountain in the world, Makalu I, soars 7,504 feet above Alaska's Mount McKinley, the highest mountain the United States. Mount McKinley is 20,320 feet high.

How tall is Makalu I? _____

Lhotse 1 is the fourth tallest mountain in the world. It's 293 feet taller than Mount McKinley (see above) and Mount Kosciusko combined! Mount Kosciusko, the highest mountain in Australia, is 7,310 feet high.

How tall is Lhotse 1? _____

Addition & Subtraction

In 1797, a man named Andre-Jacques Gamerin jumped out of a hot-air balloon while it was 3,000 feet off the ground. He was testing his new invention, the parachute. (Lucky for him, it worked!) Gamerin would have had to send the balloon up another 25,208 feet to reach the height of the third highest mountain peak in the world, Kanchenjunga.

How tall is Kanchenjunga? _____

K2, in Pakistan, is the second highest mountain in the world. It's the only one of the five tallest mountains not found in Nepal. K2 is only 42 feet higher than Kanchenjunga. How tall is K2? Hint: Use your sum from the last equation.

_____

A mountain on Mars, believed to be the tallest one in the solar system, is about four times as tall as than the tallest mountain in Africa. That African mountain, Mount Kilimanjaro, stands 19,340 feet tall. About how tall is the mountain on Mars? Hint: Add the height of Mount Kilimanjaro four times.

_____

Numbers in the News

Choose from the numbers in the boxes to finish the stories.
Hint: You can use each number choice only once.

Gum Chewer Gets Chewed Out!

| KL6249 |
| 112 |
| $439.83 |
| 3 |
| 911 |
| 50 |

Nosy Netty dialed _____ after seeing a truck

speed down her street. It was going over _____

miles an hour. Later, _____ miles out of town, the police

stopped a truck with the license plate _____ . Not only was the

truck speeding, said the arresting officer. It also contained _____

boxes of stolen gum balls, worth a total of _____ .

Snow News Is Good News

90   0   6   75   3:00   3   6:00

A record _____ feet of snow fell in sunny Sun City on Monday. "I could

barely see out my window, the snow was piled so high!" said local resident

Dee Frost. The temperature in Sun City is usually between _____ and _____

degrees Fahrenheit. But as the snow fell, so did the temperature —

dropping as low as _____ degrees Fahrenheit. The snow began

falling at _____ P.M., and didn't stop until

_____ P.M., _____ hours later. "At least

the kids are on summer break, so

they won't miss any school," said

their teacher Luke Warm.

For Sale

Used _____ -door sports car — complete with

_____ brand-new tires.

Still in good condition, after _____ miles!

It's a steal at _____!

Call _____ for more information.

| 83,000 |
| 4 |
| $4,500 |
| 555-2037 |
| 2 |

| 1918 | 12 | 5,000 | 4 | 6:30 |
| | 9th | 16 | 86 | |

Hitter Comes Through in a Pinch

An estimated _____ fans attended last night's big baseball game

between the Denver Digits and the Nevada Numbers. The

game, which began at _____ P.M., lasted _____ hours.

"The last time I saw such a close game was in _____,"

stated town old-timer Ma Fritchet. "Then again, I think that

was the last game I ever went to," the _____ -year-old-

woman admitted.

At the bottom of the _____ inning, the score was tied

and the bases loaded. Then Nevada's favorite

pinch hitter, Hetta Miss, hit a home-run, pulling her

team ahead for a final score of _____ to _____.

Addition & Subtraction 69

Number Magic

A. In a magic square like this one, you can add the numbers down, across, or diagonally. They all have the same sum. What's the magic sum in this magic square? _____

4	9	2
3	5	7
8	1	6

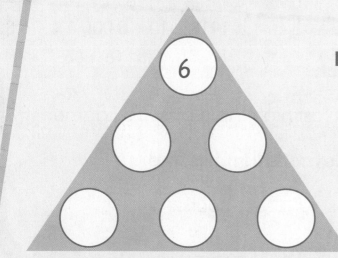

B. Fill in the circles in this magic triangle with the numbers 1 to 6. The numbers on each side of the shape should add up to 11.

C. In this magic spider, each row of digits placed diagonally will add up to 12 when you write the digits 0 to 8 where they belong.

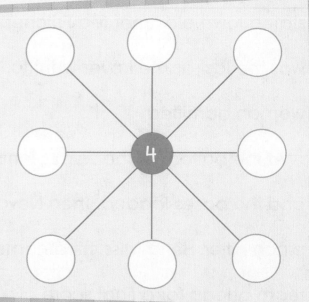

D. The only numbers you can use in this magic square are 3, 5, 6, and 13. Each row, column, and diagonal should add up to 27.

	5		
		3	
6			
			13

E. This magic square should contain the numbers 10 through 25, and each row column, and diagonal should add up to 70. The four numbers in the center square will add up to 70, too!

25			12
	16		15
13		10	24

F. Now see if you can complete this magic square. It should contain the numbers 1 to 25, and have a magic total of 65.

1	13		25	23
		11		
22	19			2
5			20	17
	7		4	14

Tic-Tac-Math

Here is a game that's similar to tic-tac-toe.
Instead of using **x**'s and **o**'s, you play with numbers instead!

You Need
- a partner • paper and pencil

1. Draw blank tic-tac-toe boards like the one shown
on this page.

2. Take turns filling in a number in one of the squares. Here are
the rules:
- You can use only the numbers 1 to 9.
- Each number can be used only once.
- The first player to go may *not* enter a number
in the center square.

3. The goal is to complete a row, column, or diagonal so that
two of the numbers add up to the third number. The order
doesn't matter. So all of these would be winning games:

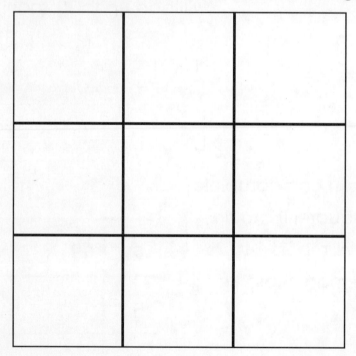

Once you get good at the game, try playing it
with the numbers 0 to 12 instead!

Addition & Subtraction Answer Key

Note: Answers read across, per page.

28–29 3, 2, 1; 1, 1, 2; 4, 1, 3; 2, 2, 4; 2, 3, 5; 2, 4, 6; 5, 2, 7; 8, 0, 8; 7, 2, 9; 6, 4, 10; equations may vary but should equal 11.

30–31 40, 70, 80, 120, 150; 44, 74, 114, 134; 52, 62, 82, 122; 100, 420, 660, 780, 785; 80, 161, 100, 675, 62, 862, 61, 1,475, 119, 3,274

32–33 16, 23, 75, 48, 61, 90, 117, 107, 215, 534; can't see you.

34–35 27, 67, 112, 45, 26, 80, 93, 60, 140; hare-plane

36–37 1. 21/Bee Lick, Kentucky, 2. 38/Burnt Corn, Alabama, 3. 32/Embarrass, Wisconsin, 4. 91/Fleatown, Ohio, 5. 90/Gnaw Bone, Indiana, 6. 82/Hungry Horse, Montana, 7. 120/Peculiar, Missouri, 8. 101/Worms, Nebraska, 9. 170/Ninety Six, South Carolina, 10. 121/Odd, West Virginia

38–39 326, 967, 431, 758, 821, 706, 1,017, 292, 155, 938, 780, 468; 3, 1, 7, 5, 2, 5

40–41 629, 847, 30, 91, 672, 63, 47,883, 72,810, 2,164, 3,245, 96,472, 86,492, 68, 511, 29, 43,586, 743, 23, 90, 852, 48, 479, 98,246, 18,178, 6,246, 38,549, 362, 728, 915, 523

42–43 52 +12 or 12 + 52 = 64, 18 + 15 or 15 + 18 = 33, 17 + 63 or 63 + 17 = 80, 41 + 41 = 82, 14 + 22 or 22 + 14 = 36

44–45 **See below.**

46–47 2, 23, 10, 202, 29, 47, 78, 55, 9, 290, 19, 489; 3, 9, 4

48–49 219 – 6 = 213, 478 – 19 = 459, 389 – 95 = 294, 48 – 6 = 42, 82 – 13 = 69, 411 – 16 = 395, 558 – 89 = 469, 880 – 416 = 464, 708 – 98 = 610, 712 – 106 = 606, 726 – 708 = 18, 629 – 114 = 515

50–51 1927: television, 1886: talking doll, 1876: telephone, 1973: the Internet, 1762: sandwich, 1898: flashlight, 1565: pencil, 1948: Velcro, 1890: zipper, 1853: potato chips; fill in timeline as directed.

52–53 hands: 38, shoulders: 4, head: 29, chest: 25, wrists: 16, arms: 6, legs: 8, ankles: 14, hips: 2, back: 26, feet: 38; 206

54–55 Answers will vary; **circle:** e, n, i, n; **underline:** n, c, s, t, e; nine cents

56–57 subtract, round, tens, sum, difference, equals, estimate, even, odd, ones; **see below.**

58–59 e = 29, r ≠ 12, h = 82, r ≠ 23, t = 23, r ≠ 44, r ≠ 51, c = 70, e = 62, h = 32, a = 66, r ≠ 69, cheetah

60–61 Numbers on clouds should match number written on plane.

62–63 1. Houston and San Diego; 2. 1,490 miles; 3. Atlanta and Houston; 4. 791 miles; 5. 1,830 miles; 6. 1,645 miles; 7. 18 miles; 8. 232 miles; 9. 7,564 miles

64–65 32, 33, 7, 25 minutes, 597, 297, 18

66–67 33,476 – 4,448 = 29,028 feet, 7,504 + 20,320 = 27,824 feet, 293 + 20,230 + 7,731 = 27,923, 3,000 + 25,208 = 28,208 feet, 28,208 + 42 = 28,250; 19,340 + 19,340 +19,340 +19,340 = 77,360

68–69 911, 50, 3, KL6249, 112, $439.83; 6, 75, 90, 0, 3:00, 6:00, 3; 2, 4, 83,000, $4,500, 555-2037; 5,000, 6:30, 4, 1918, 86, 9th, 16, 12

70–71 A. 15; **see below**

44–45

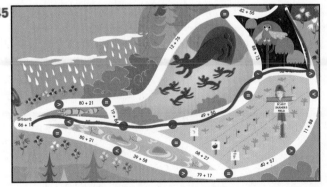

70–71

3	5	13	6
13	6	3	5
6	13	5	3
5	3	6	13

14	20	17	19
25	11	22	12
18	16	21	15
13	23	10	24

1	13	3	25	23
21	18	11	6	9
22	19	12	10	2
5	8	15	20	17
16	7	24	4	14

56–57

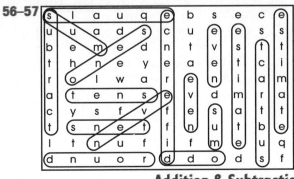

Cool Patterns

When a number is added to itself, it creates a list of **multiples**.

Examples

Multiples of 2 include 2, 4, 6, and 8.

Multiples of 5 include 5, 10, 25, 20.

The list of multiples for any number (except 0) is infinite. It can go on and on forever!

1	2	3	4	5	6	7	8	9	10
11	12	13	14	15	16	17	18	19	20
21	22	23	24	25	26	27	28	29	30
31	32	33	34	35	36	37	38	39	40
41	42	43	44	45	46	47	48	49	50
51	52	53	54	55	56	57	58	59	60
61	62	63	64	65	66	67	68	69	70
71	72	73	74	75	76	77	78	79	80
81	82	83	84	85	86	87	88	89	90
91	92	93	94	95	96	97	98	99	100

Color all the multiples of 10 **red**.
What pattern do you see?

_____

Color all the multiples of 11 green.
What pattern do you see?

_____

1	2	3	4	5	6	7	8	9	10
11	12	13	14	15	16	17	18	19	20
21	22	23	24	25	26	27	28	29	30
31	32	33	34	35	36	37	38	39	40
41	42	43	44	45	46	47	48	49	50
51	52	53	54	55	56	57	58	59	60
61	62	63	64	65	66	67	68	69	70
71	72	73	74	75	76	77	78	79	80
81	82	83	84	85	86	87	88	89	90
91	92	93	94	95	96	97	98	99	100

Color all the multiples of 5 **black**.
What pattern do you see?

1	2	3	4	5	6	7	8	9	10
11	12	13	14	15	16	17	18	19	20
21	22	23	24	25	26	27	28	29	30
31	32	33	34	35	36	37	38	39	40
41	42	43	44	45	46	47	48	49	50
51	52	53	54	55	56	57	58	59	60
61	62	63	64	65	66	67	68	69	70
71	72	73	74	75	76	77	78	79	80
81	82	83	84	85	86	87	88	89	90
91	92	93	94	95	96	97	98	99	100

Color all the multiples of 3 **yellow**.
What pattern do you see?

1	2	3	4	5	6	7	8	9	10
11	12	13	14	15	16	17	18	19	20
21	22	23	24	25	26	27	28	29	30
31	32	33	34	35	36	37	38	39	40
41	42	43	44	45	46	47	48	49	50
51	52	53	54	55	56	57	58	59	60
61	62	63	64	65	66	67	68	69	70
71	72	73	74	75	76	77	78	79	80
81	82	83	84	85	86	87	88	89	90
91	92	93	94	95	96	97	98	99	100

Color all the odd numbers **purple**.
What pattern do you see?

1	2	3	4	5	6	7	8	9	10
11	12	13	14	15	16	17	18	19	20
21	22	23	24	25	26	27	28	29	30
31	32	33	34	35	36	37	38	39	40
41	42	43	44	45	46	47	48	49	50
51	52	53	54	55	56	57	58	59	60
61	62	63	64	65	66	67	68	69	70
71	72	73	74	75	76	77	78	79	80
81	82	83	84	85	86	87	88	89	90
91	92	93	94	95	96	97	98	99	100

Color all the numbers with digits adding up to more than 9 **orange**.
What pattern do you see?

1	2	3	4	5	6	7	8	9	10
11	12	13	14	15	16	17	18	19	20
21	22	23	24	25	26	27	28	29	30
31	32	33	34	35	36	37	38	39	40
41	42	43	44	45	46	47	48	49	50
51	52	53	54	55	56	57	58	59	60
61	62	63	64	65	66	67	68	69	70
71	72	73	74	75	76	77	78	79	80
81	82	83	84	85	86	87	88	89	90
91	92	93	94	95	96	97	98	99	100

Multiplication Riddles

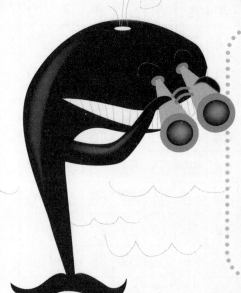

Remember: An **x** between two numbers means "multiply." When you multiply two numbers, the answer is called the **product**. You can read the **x** as "times."
Example: 2 × 3 is the same as two times three.

A **times table** is a list of multiplication equations that all have one number the same.
Example: 2 × 0, 2 × 1, and 2 × 3 all belong to the two times table.

Solve the equations in each multiplication table.

Five Times Table	Four Times Table	Six Times Table
5 × 2 = _____ s	4 × 2 = _____ n	6 × 2 = _____ i
5 × 3 = _____ f	4 × 3 = _____ a	6 × 3 = _____ h
5 × 4 = _____ h	4 × 4 = _____ d	6 × 4 = _____ s
5 × 5 = _____ i		6 × 5 = _____ p
		6 × 6 = _____ c

Use the letters next to your answers to solve this riddle. The letters in the first word come from the five times table; the second word from the four times table; the third word from the six times table.

What's a whale's favorite lunch?

_____ _____ _____ _____   _____ _____ _____
15   25   10   20   12   8   16

_____ _____ _____ _____ _____
36   18   12   30   24

Three Times Table   Seven Times Table

$3 \times 2 =$ _____ i $7 \times 2 =$ _____ i $7 \times 4 =$ _____ l $7 \times 6 =$ _____ s

$3 \times 3 =$ _____ t $7 \times 3 =$ _____ p $7 \times 5 =$ _____ s $7 \times 7 =$ _____ t

The letters in the first word come from the three times table; the second word from the seven times table.

What does a banana do when it hears ice scream?

___ ___   ___ ___ ___ ___ ___ ___
 6   9   42   21   28   14   49   35

Eight Times Table

$8 \times 2 =$ _____ o $8 \times 4 =$ _____ l $8 \times 6 =$ _____ a $8 \times 8 =$ _____ e

$8 \times 3 =$ _____ b $8 \times 5 =$ _____ t $8 \times 7 =$ _____ g

Use the letters next to your answers to solve the riddle below.

What do you call a young turkey?

___   ___ ___ ___ ___ ___ ___
48   56   16   24   32   64   40

Nine Times Table

Use the letters next to your answers to solve the riddle below.

$9 \times 2 =$ _____ s

$9 \times 3 =$ _____ g

What do you have if you have 6 apples in one hand and 9 apples in the other?

$9 \times 4 =$ _____ d

$9 \times 5 =$ _____ h

___ ___ ___
63   72   27

$9 \times 6 =$ _____ a

$9 \times 7 =$ _____ b

___ ___ ___ ___ ___
45   54   81   36   18

$9 \times 8 =$ _____ i

$9 \times 9 =$ _____ n

The Grid Game

An **array** is a grid that helps you see what happens when you multiply.

This array shows 3 rows of 4 squares.

It shows that 3 × 4 = 12.

It also shows that 3 × 4 = 4 × 3.

Count to see how.

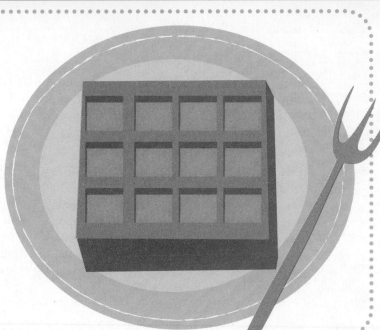

Solve these multiplication equations.

13 × 2 = _____   6 × 2 = _____

3 × 5 = _____   3 × 11 = _____

7 × 4 = _____   2 × 3 = _____

6 × 9 = _____   11 × 8 = _____

7 × 7 = _____   5 × 5 = _____

Now use different color crayons or markers to create arrays showing all 10 of the multiplication equations on page 78 on this giant waffle grid.

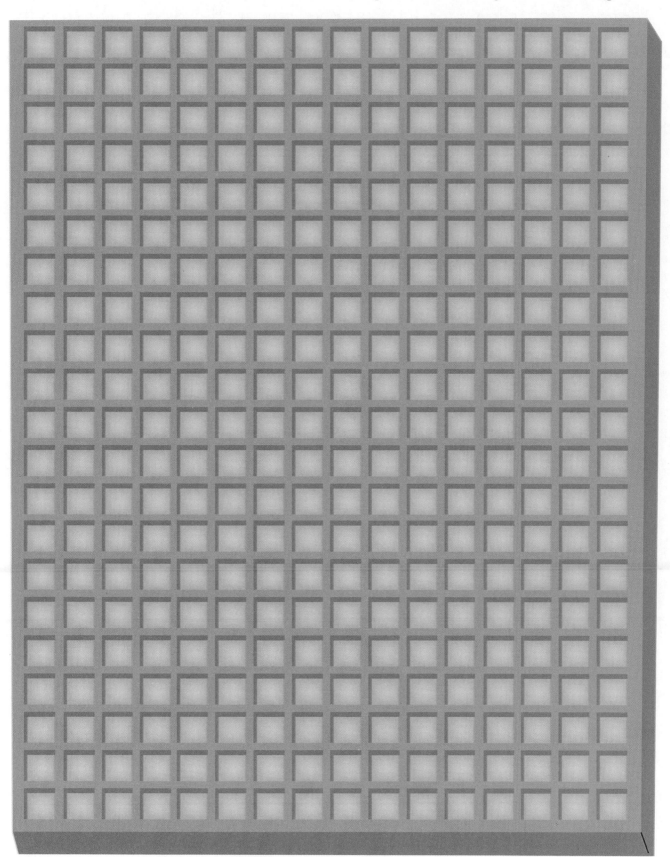

Multiplying Animals

Groups of animals often have a name. Use multiplication to match each animal with its group name. Multiply. Look at the box if you need help.

To multiply a multi-digit number by a single-digit number, you may have to regroup. Here's how.

1. Multiply the ones. Write down the product so the ones column lines up. If the product is greater than 9, carry any value of 10 or more into the tens column.

$$\begin{array}{r} \overset{1}{6}2 \\ \times\ 6 \\ \hline 2 \end{array}$$

2. Multiply the single digit by the original number in the tens column. If you carried a value from the ones column, add that to your new product. Write the total in the tens column. If the value is greater than one digit, the remaining value gets carried to the hundreds column.

$$\begin{array}{r} \overset{1}{6}2 \\ \times\ 6 \\ \hline 372 \end{array}$$

Think: (6 × 6) + 1 = 37

$$\begin{array}{r} 132 \\ \times\ \ 3 \\ \hline \end{array}$$

baboons

$$\begin{array}{r} 728 \\ \times\ \ 6 \\ \hline \end{array}$$

kangaroos

869
× 1

toads

242
× 3

oysters

821
× 2

cattle

432
× 4

turkeys

690
× 5

crows

129
× 3

parrots

181
× 2

ponies

869 a knot   396 a tribe

3,450 a murder   1,642 a drove

362 a string   387 a company

4,368 a troop   1,728 a rafter

726 a bed

Multiplication Rules!

A math rule is called a **property**. Multiplication, like addition, has a **commutative property**. That means the order in which you multiply numbers does not change the product.

Examples

$$5 + 8 = 13$$
$$8 + 5 = 13$$
$$5 \times 8 = 40$$
$$8 \times 5 = 40$$

Write letters in the boxes to match the equations that are equal because of their commutative property. This will tell you where some wacky laws really are—or once were—in law books!

$$\begin{array}{r} 71 \\ + 1 \\ \hline \end{array}$$

a Pennsylvania

$$\begin{array}{r} 60 \\ + 12 \\ \hline \end{array}$$

b Hawaii

$$\begin{array}{r} 12 \\ \times 6 \\ \hline \end{array}$$

c Michigan

$$\begin{array}{r} 9 \\ \times 8 \\ \hline \end{array}$$

d New Jersey

$$\begin{array}{r} 36 \\ \times 2 \\ \hline \end{array}$$

e California

$$\begin{array}{r} 17 \\ + 55 \\ \hline \end{array}$$

f Kentucky

$$\begin{array}{r} 69 \\ + 3 \\ \hline \end{array}$$

g South Carolina

$$\begin{array}{r} 45 \\ + 27 \\ \hline \end{array}$$

h West Virginia

$$\begin{array}{r} 24 \\ \times 3 \\ \hline \end{array}$$

i Oregon

$$\begin{array}{r} 18 \\ \times 4 \\ \hline \end{array}$$

j Alaska

$$\begin{array}{r} 48 \\ + 24 \\ \hline \end{array}$$

k Texas

$$\begin{array}{r} 1 \\ \times 72 \\ \hline \end{array}$$

l New Hampshire

☐ 8 × 9 It's illegal to slurp your soup in a public eating place.

☐ 3 × 24 It is illegal to eat ice cream on Sundays.

☐ 4 × 18 It is an offense to push a live moose out of a moving airplane.

☐ 2 × 36 It's illegal for a woman to drive while wearing a bathrobe.

☐ 1 + 71 It is illegal to sleep on top of a refrigerator outdoors.

☐ 12 + 60 It is not permitted to place coins in one's ears.

☐ 55 + 17 It is illegal to fish with a bow and arrow.

☐ 24 + 48 It is illegal to milk another person's cow.

☐ 3 + 69 It is not permitted to keep horses in bathtubs.

☐ 6 × 12 It is not permitted for a woman to cut her own hair without her husband's permission.

☐ 72 × 1 It is illegal to pick up seaweed off the beach at certain hours.

☐ 27 + 45 It is prohibited to whistle underwater.

What do these equations all have in common? Hint: You have to find the sums or products to find out.

_____

No Business Like Shoe Business!

The Lucky Horse Shoe Shop now sells shoes for ostriches, ladybugs, spiders, and lobsters, too! Figure out how many shoes each set of customers will need.

Ostriches have 2 legs.

Spiders have 8 legs.

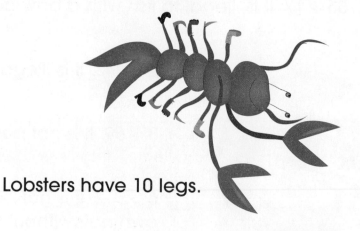

Lobsters have 10 legs.

Ladybugs have 6 legs.

Horses have 4 legs.

6 ostriches will need _____ × _____ = _____ shoes.

7 spiders will need _____ × _____ = _____ shoes.

10 lobsters will need _____ × _____ = _____ shoes.

4 horses and 2 lobsters will need

(_____ × _____) + (_____ × _____) = _____ + _____ = _____ shoes.

3 spiders and 4 ladybugs will need

(_____ × _____) + (_____ × _____) = _____ + _____ = _____ shoes.

10 horses, 5 ostriches, and 6 lobsters will need

(_____ × _____) + (_____ × _____) + (_____ × _____) =

_____ + _____ + _____ = _____ shoes.

How many pairs of shoes will 5 horses and 12 ostriches need?

(_____ × _____) + (_____ × _____) = _____ + _____ = _____

A type of centipede found in southern Europe has 177 pairs of legs. That's more legs than any other type of animal ever found! How many shoes would 3 of these centipedes, plus 3 horses, 3 ladybugs, and 3 lobsters need? Write the equation first.

_____

The Whole Tooth About Multiplication

Solve the multiplication equations to find out
how many teeth each adult animal has.

walrus: 3 × 6 = _____

elephant: 6 × 1 = _____

otter: 6 × 6 = _____

baleen whale: 0 × 7 = _____

sea otter: 4 × 8 = _____

cat: 6 × 5 = _____

jackrabbit: 4 × 7 = _____

porcupine:
10 × 2 = _____

mouse: 4 × 4 = _____

pig: 11 × 4 = _____

skunk: 17 × 2 = _____

squirrel: 2 × 11 = _____

opossum: 25 × 2 = _____

polar bear: 7 × 6 = _____

raccoon: 8 × 5 = _____

Zeroing In

What kinds of things happen in a typical minute, hour, day, or year? Read each word problem. Then write a multiplication equation, and find the product. The math tip in the box will help you.

1. Look at the multiplication equation. If there is a 0 at the end of one of the numbers, drop it. For example, to multiply

$$\begin{array}{r} 8\,1 \\ \times\ 7\,0 \\ \hline \end{array}$$

think

$$\begin{array}{r} 8\,1 \\ \times\ 7 \\ \hline 5\,6\,7 \end{array}$$

2. Then put your 0 back in to the right of the ones column in your answer. So,

$$\begin{array}{r} 8\,1 \\ \times\ 7\,0 \\ \hline 5{,}6\,7\,0 \end{array}$$

The average teen spends about 40 minutes a day on the phone. How many minutes is that in a week?

$$\begin{array}{r} 4\,0 \\ \times\ 7 \\ \hline \end{array}$$

Americans eat about 100 acres of pizza each day. How many acres of pizza is that in a year? Hint: A year equals 365 days.

$$\times\ \underline{\hspace{2cm}}$$

About 10,000 babies are born in the United States every day. How many babies is that in a year?

×_____

A small drip from a leaky faucet can waste 50 gallons of water a day. How many gallons is that in a year?

×_____

A cheetah can run as fast as 70 miles in 1 hour. If the big cat didn't take a break, how many miles would it run in 24 hours, or 1 day?

×_____

An average cow produces about 40 glasses of milk a day. About how many glasses is that in a year?

×_____

×_____

A machine makes about 360,000 feet of toilet paper every hour. How many feet of toilet paper is that in a day?

License to Multiply

What motto is found on each of these license plates? Solve the multiplication equations and look for the product in the box to find out.

DELAWARE
2 × 55
_____

MAINE
15 × 6
_____

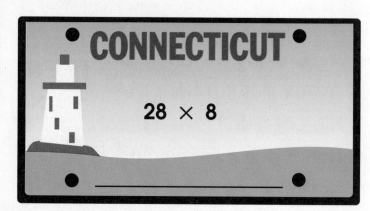
CONNECTICUT
28 × 8
_____

ONTARIO
48 × 4
_____

NORTH CAROLINA
7 × 19
_____

MISSOURI

13 × 9

_____

EXPLORE **Minnesota**

3 × 26

_____

ALASKA

68 × 4

_____

NEW MEXICO

14 × 9

_____

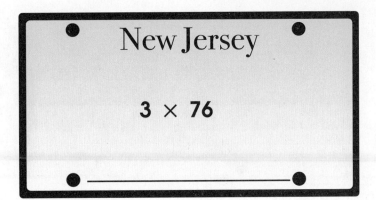

New Jersey

3 × 76

_____

272 The Last Frontier   90 Vacationland

126 Land of Enchantment   78 10,000 Lakes

133 First in Flight   117 Show-Me State

192 Yours to Discover   224 Constitution State

228 Garden State   110 The First State

One for You, One for Me

Split these candies evenly among the kids shown. Then write an equation beneath each group to show how you divided them.

_____ ÷ _____ = _____

_____ ÷ _____ = _____

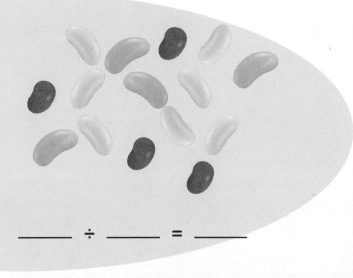

_____ ÷ _____ = _____

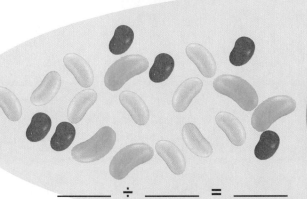

_____ ÷ _____ = _____

_____ ÷ _____ = _____

Now solve these division equations.

8 ÷ 4 = _____   21 ÷ 3 = _____

12 ÷ 3 = _____   16 ÷ 4 = _____

15 ÷ 3 = _____

Math Opposites

Multiplication and division are **inverse**, or opposite, operations.

That means you can check division equations with multiplication.

For example:

$$2\overline{)64} = 32 \qquad 32 \times 2 = 64$$

You can also check multiplication equations with division.

For example,

$$15 \times 4 = 60 \qquad 4\overline{)60} = 15$$

Write the inverse equations for the equations below.
Compare the answers. If the first equation is **not true**,
change the **=** (equals) to **≠** (not equal to).
Circle the letters next to any **true** equations.

r $25 \div 5 = 6$ _____

e $16 \times 3 = 48$ _____

r $12 \times 7 = 87$ _____

h $39 \div 3 = 15$ _____

r $72 \div 9 = 8$ _____

r $14 \times 4 = 66$ _____

b $8 \times 56 = 448$ _____

r $936 \div 9 = 103$ _____

e $6 \times 82 = 493$ _____

a $840 \div 4 = 210$ _____

r $23 \times 6 = 138$ _____

b $132 \div 11 = 12$ _____

Unscramble the letters you circled to answer this riddle.

Who can shave 25 times a day and still have a beard?

A ____ ____ ____ ____ ____ ____!

Doggy Division

Where does this pup like to spend his time?
Divide. Then connect the dots in number order.

Hint: To solve a division equation, it
sometimes helps to think of the inverse.

For example:
to solve $40 \div 10$, think: $10 \times ? = 40$.
The answer is 4.

$23 \div 23 =$

$18 \div 9 =$

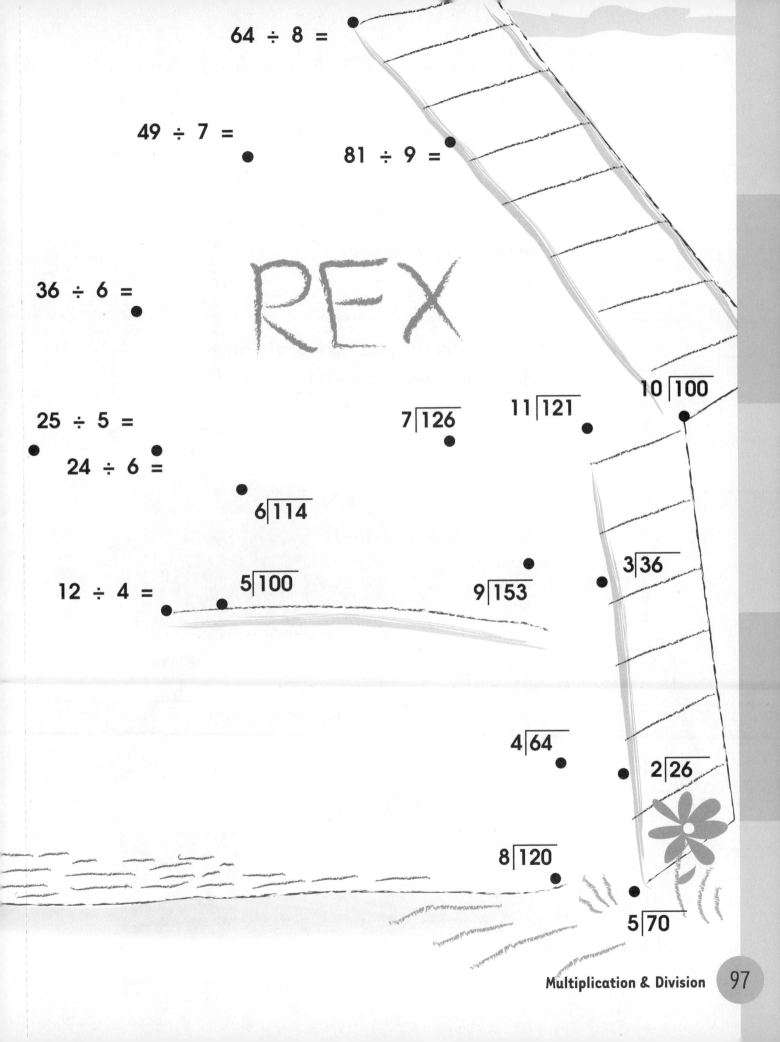

64 ÷ 8 =

49 ÷ 7 =

81 ÷ 9 =

36 ÷ 6 =

REX

25 ÷ 5 =

24 ÷ 6 =

$7\overline{)126}$

$11\overline{)121}$

$10\overline{)100}$

$6\overline{)114}$

$3\overline{)36}$

12 ÷ 4 =

$5\overline{)100}$

$9\overline{)153}$

$4\overline{)64}$

$2\overline{)26}$

$8\overline{)120}$

$5\overline{)70}$

Seesaw Math

Use division to figure out these equations. The math tip in the box will help you. Write your equation and answer for each question.

> **1.** Look at the division equation. If there is a 0 at the end of one of the numbers, drop it. For example, to divide
>
> $250 \div 5$
>
> think: $25 \div 5 = 5$.
>
> **2.** Then put the 0 to the right of the ones column in your answer. So,
>
> $250 \div 5 = 50$.

African elephant 11,000 pounds

parrot 2 pounds

Jack Russell terrier 10 pounds

cat 8 pounds

rabbit 5 pounds

ostrich 250 pounds

How many parrots would it take to balance the Jack Russell terrier on a seesaw? _____

How many parrots would it take to balance the cat?

_____

How many rabbits would it take to balance the ostrich? _____

How many parrots would it take to balance 3 cats?

_____

How many Jack Russell terriers would it take to balance 2 ostriches? _____

An African elephant is one of the heaviest land mammals on earth! To balance this elephant on a seesaw,

How many Jack Russell terriers would it take? _____

How many parrots would it take? _____

How many cats would it take? _____

How many rabbits would it take? _____

How many ostriches would it take? _____

Multiples and Factors to the Finish

A list of **multiples** is created by adding a number to itself.
Multiples of 2 include 2, 4, 6, and 8.

Clues

Multiples of 5 can move ahead 1 space.

Multiples of 7 can move ahead 1 space.

Multiples of 6 can move ahead 1 space.

Numbers that are *not* multiples of 2 can move ahead 1 space.

Factors of 100 can move ahead 1 space.

Help the runners get to the finish line.
Add an **x** to the lane for each space that a runner can move, based on the directions below. The runner to reach the finish line first wins!

A **factor** is a number that when multiplied by another number (another factor) equals a given product. Factors of 12 include 1, 2, 3, 4, 6, and 12.

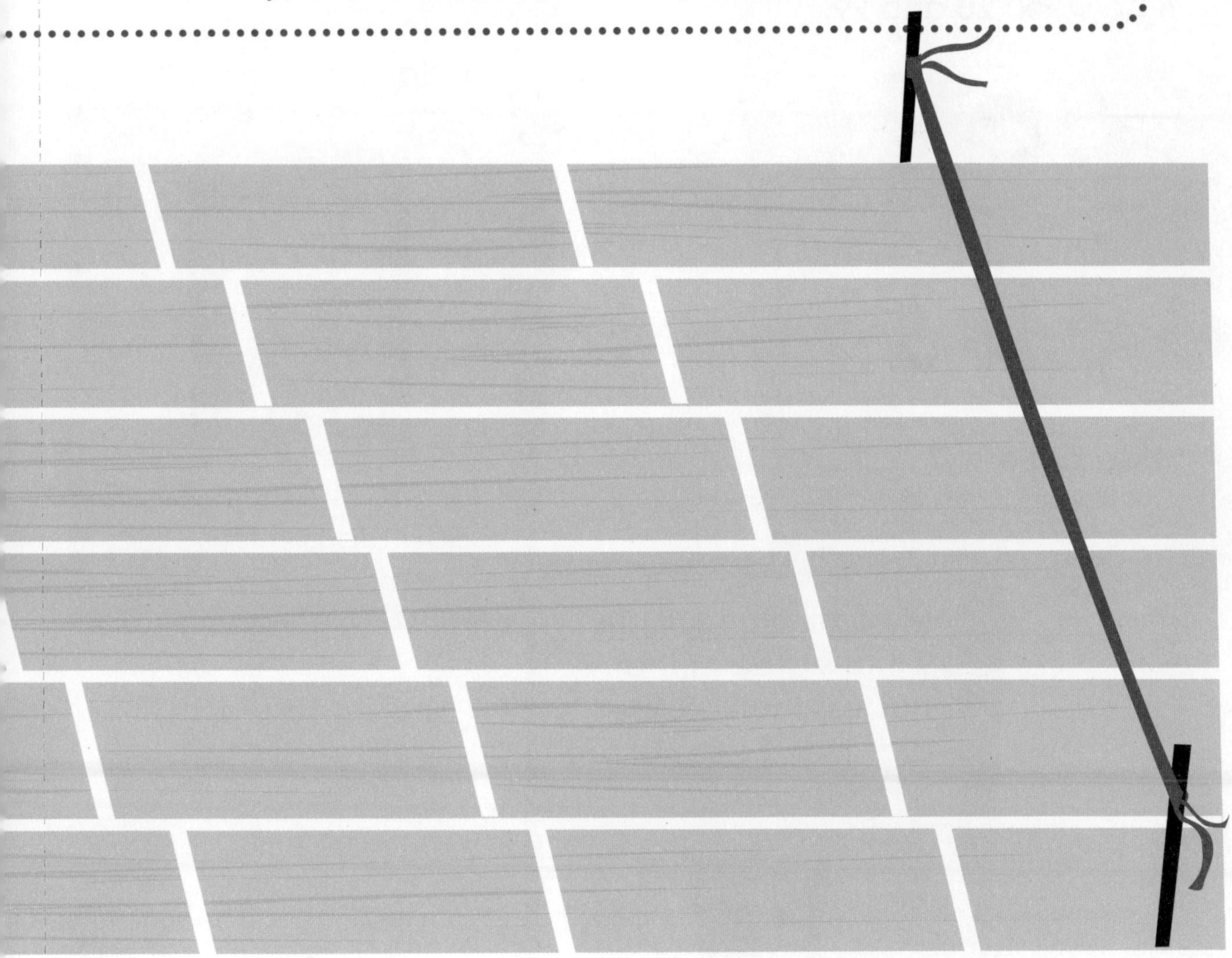

Numbers that are factors of both 4 and 8 can move ahead 2 spaces.
Numbers that are factors of both 3 and 9 can move ahead 2 spaces.

Which runner wins? _____

How Old Am I?

Use the clues to figure out each person's age. Write the answer.
Hint: Start by writing numbers that fit the first part of the clue.
Then cross out ones that don't fit the other parts.

My age is a multiple of 6 between 20 and 29.

How old am I? _____

My age is between 10 and 60. When you multiply the digits in my age, you get 21.

How old am I? _____

My age is a multiple of 9 that's greater than 9 but less than 45. The digit in the ones place is less than 7.

How old am I? _____

My age is an even number between 50 and 80. It's a multiple of 5 and 6.

How old am I? _____

My age is an odd number between 50 and 70. It can be evenly divided by both 7 and 3, and its first digit is even.

How old am I? _____

My age is less than 58. It's a multiple of 8, and if you add 1, that number is a multiple of 7.

How old am I? _____

My age is less than 100 and more than 50. It can be divided evenly by 2, and it's a factor of 282.

How old am I? _____

Clever Coloring

A French mathematician, Blaise Pascal, created this clever math triangle more than 300 years ago. Follow the directions to see what patterns you can find in it.

Color all of the numbers that can be evenly divided by 3 **red**.

Color all of the numbers that can be evenly divided by 5 **purple**.

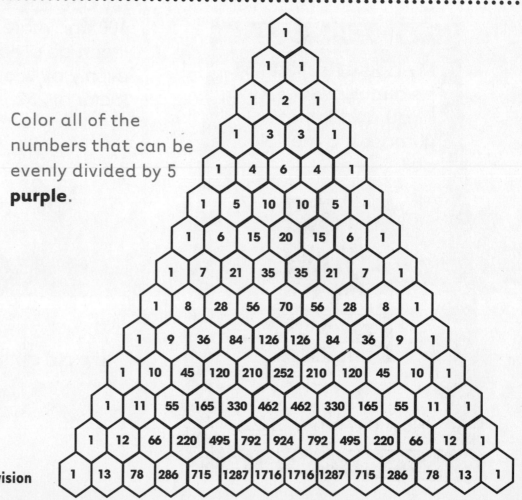

Color all of the numbers that can be evenly divided by 7 **green**.

The numbers you used —3, 5, and 7—are **prime numbers**. Prime numbers have only two factors. They can be divided evenly only by the number itself or 1.

Example: You can write only 3 ÷ 3 or 3 ÷ 1.

What is the next prime number after 7?

_____

Hint: It is > 9 but < 12. Color all the numbers divisible by this prime number **blue**.

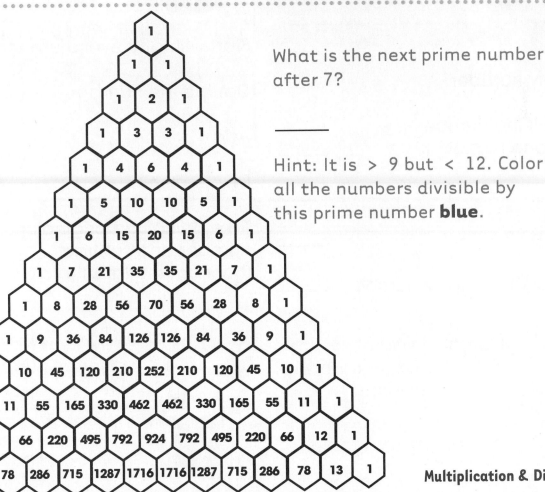

Math Magic

What's the magic total? Follow the math steps below to find out!

Pick any number. _____

Multiply it by 4. _____

Add 12. _____

Divide by 2. _____

Subtract twice the original number. _____

Now try it with a different number. What always happens?

_____

Pick any number. _____

Add to it the number that is one higher. _____

Add 9. _____

Divide by 2. _____

Subtract the original number. _____

Now try it with a different number. What always happens?

_____

Pick any number. _____

Multiply by 6. _____

Add 12. _____

Divide by 3. _____

Subtract twice the original number. _____

Now try it with a different number. What always happens?

_____

Start with any even number _____

Double the number. _____

Add 12. _____

Divide by 4. _____

Take half of the original number and subtract that from the latest total. _____

Now try it with a different number. What always happens?

_____

Pick any number. _____

Multiply by 3. _____

Add 8. _____

Add your original number. _____

Divide by 4. _____

Subtract your original
number. _____

Now try it with a
different number. What
always happens?

_____

Pick any number. _____

Add the number that is
one higher than your
original number. _____

Add 11. _____

Divide by 2. _____

Subtract your original number. _____

Now try it with a
different number. What
always happens?

_____

Pick any number. _____

Add 6. _____

Multiply by 3. _____

Subtract 18. _____

Divide by the number
you started with. _____

Subtract 1. _____

Now try it with a
different number. What
always happens?

_____

Pick any number. _____

Multiply by 4. _____

Add 6. _____

Multiply by 3. _____

Subtract 18. _____

Divide by 12. _____

Now try it with a
different number. What
always happens?

_____

Horsing Around with Math

Write any number on the horse's saddle. Then do the equations all along the course. The horse should get back to the number you started with when it jumps over an obstacle and when it gets to the finish line.

÷ 7 = _____

× 21 = _____

× 15 = _____

÷ 9 = _____

÷ 5 = _____

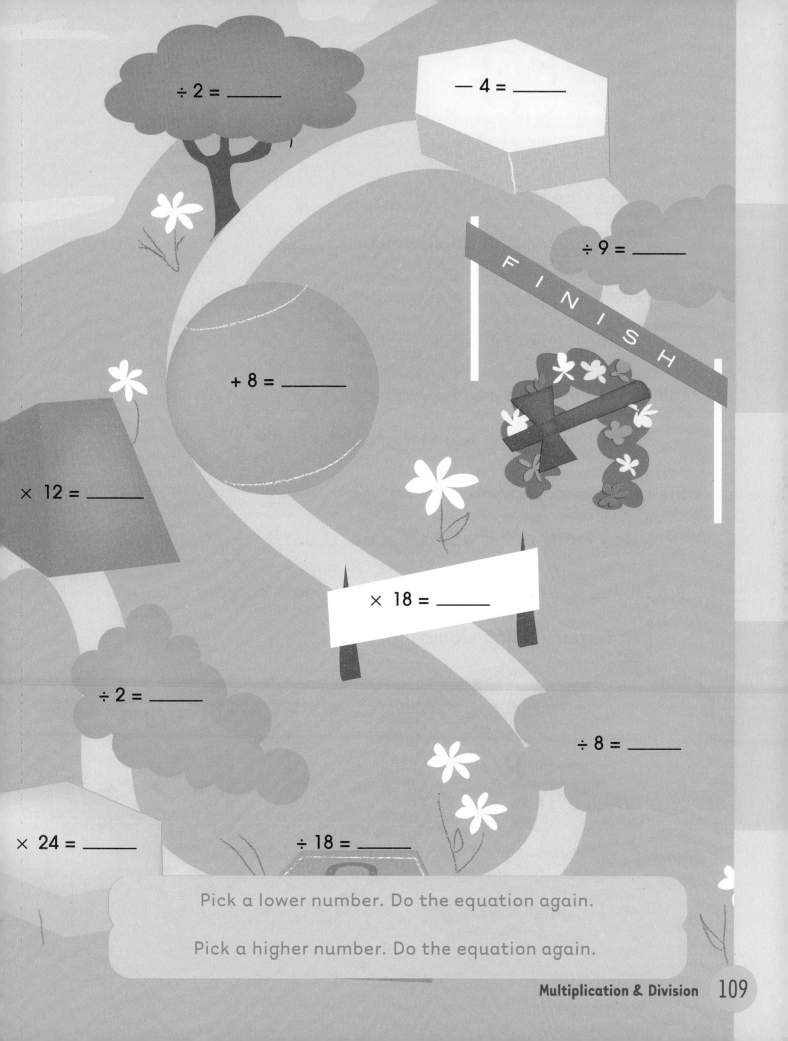

÷ 2 = _____

— 4 = _____

÷ 9 = _____

+ 8 = _____

FINISH

× 12 = _____

× 18 = _____

÷ 2 = _____

÷ 8 = _____

× 24 = _____

÷ 18 = _____

Pick a lower number. Do the equation again.

Pick a higher number. Do the equation again.

Multiplication & Division 109

A Race to the Finish

It's race day. Without going backward or crossing over any lines that you have drawn, draw a line on the the path that gives . . .

the tortoise the most points he can get.

How many points would that be? _____

the hare the most points she can get.

How many points would that be? _____

the tortoise the least points he can get.

How many points would that be? _____

the hare the least points she can get.

How many points would that be? _____

Both the tortoise and the hare have the same number of points.

How many points would that be? _____

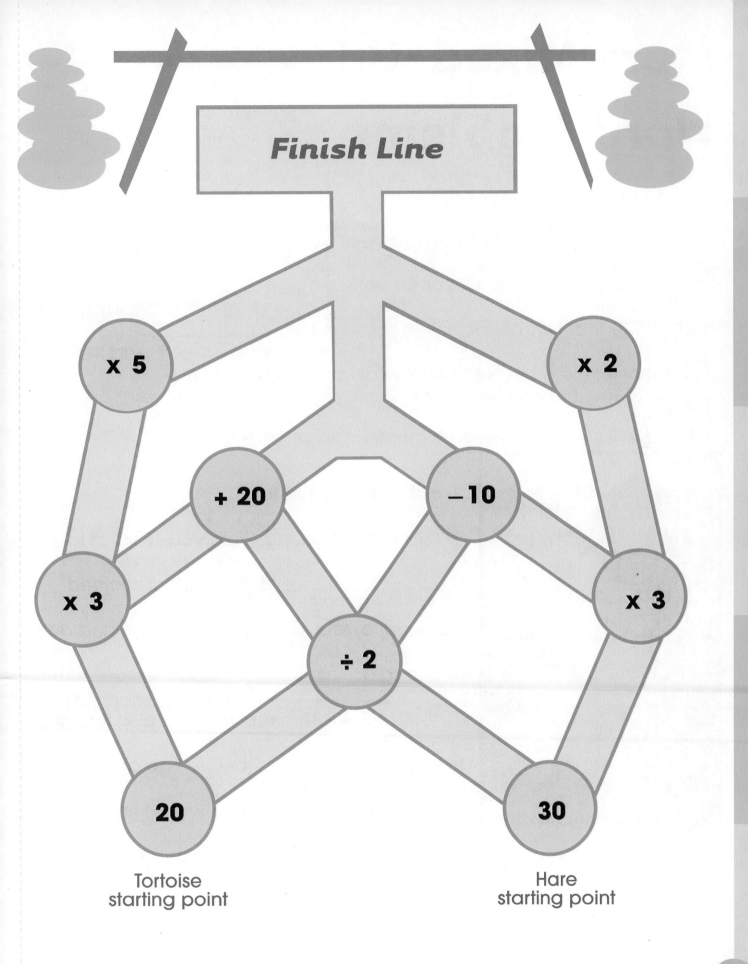

Finish Line

x 5

x 2

+ 20

−10

x 3

÷ 2

x 3

20

30

Tortoise
starting point

Hare
starting point

More Mixed-Up Word Problems

Write a word on each line as described. (Don't read the problem first!) Then read and answer each problem.

Katy Doodle's Hit Parade

Katy Doodle is a big fan of the rock group The _____.
                                                            plural noun

She always carries around 5 copies of their megahit _____
                                                    question a teacher might ask you

and 3 times that number of their latest release, _____.
                                                    something a parent might say

How many of the group's CDs does Katy carry around with

her in all? _____

Tina's Trying Tasks

"Since this morning, I told you 15 times to

_____," Tina's mother scolded.
        annoying chore

"Now go to your _____ and do
                        location

it!" she said.

"But, Mother," Tina replied, "you also told me

to _____ before I do anything
        different annoying chore

else. And you told me to do that 24 times, twice

as many times as you told me to _____. I didn't know what
                                        one more annoying chore

to do first! That's why I'm just _____. How many times
                                        doing something fun

has Tina been told to do annoying chores on this day? _____

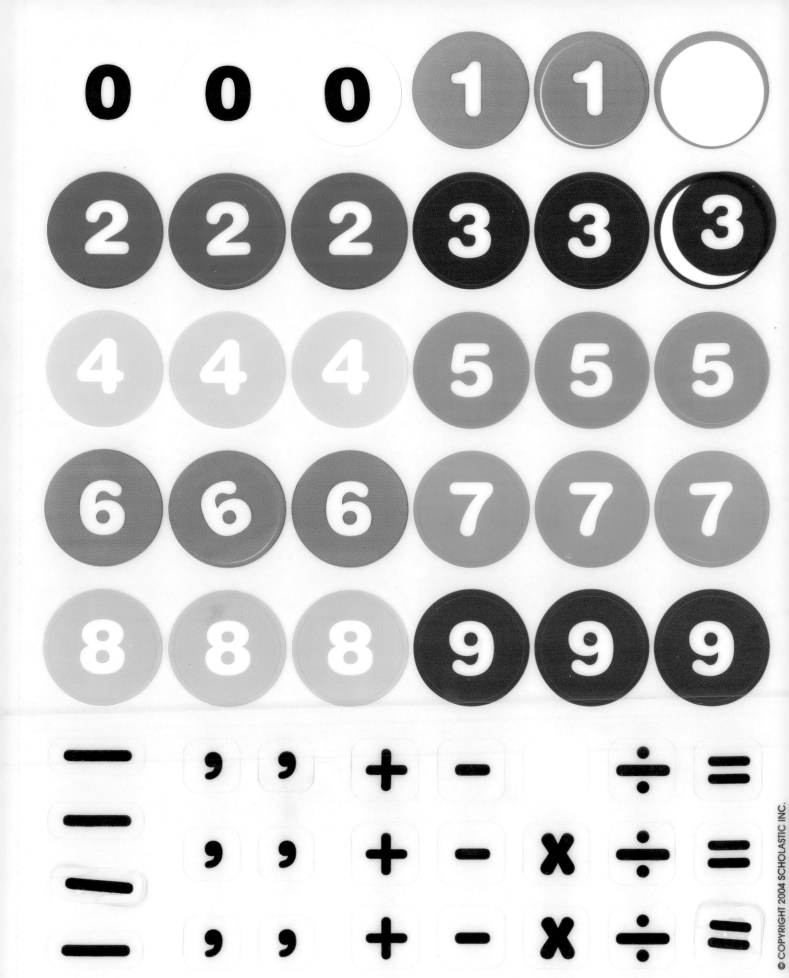

Just Three Wishes?

If you're ever lucky enough to be granted 3 wishes by a _____,
                                                            animal

use them wisely! For each wish that you use well, you will be granted 3 more.

But if you waste any wishes on something foolish, like _____,
                                                          plural noun

all your wishes will immediately disappear. How many wishes will you get

if you use the first 3 wishes wisely? _____

Share and Share Alike

Generous Jane was a _____ girl and was always willing to
                        adjective

share. One day, her aunt gave her a gift of a dozen _____.
                                                        plural noun

Jane decided to split them evenly among her and her 3 best friends. Then

her parents gave her 8 _____, and she shared those with
                            plural noun

the same friends as well. How many gifts was Jane originally given in

all? _____ After sharing, how many of her gifts did she have for

herself? _____

Let Them Eat Cake!

To celebrate his 10th birthday, Cory asks 31 of his

_____ friends over for a party. There's so much to do to get
    adjective

ready! He hangs up 18 _____ as decorations and orders a
                          plural noun

birthday cake in the shape of a _____. According to the
                                      noun

saleswoman, each cake feeds only 8 people. How many of these cakes will

Cory need to be sure he has enough for everyone, including himself?

_____

Do-It-Yourself Fast Food

At U-Do-It Fast Food, the motto is "A side of math with every order!" That means you make your own meals, and then figure out what you have to pay.

French Fries: 9 for 99¢

Pasta: 3¢ per strand

Chicken fingers: 89¢ per finger

Cookies: 5 for $1.00

Burger Buns: 15¢ each

Tomatoes: 12¢ per slice

Lettuce: 14¢ per leaf

Burger patties: 2 for $1.00

Use the menu prices to figure out the cost of the meals below. Hint: You may have to figure out an item's unit cost. A **unit cost** is how much one thing in a group costs, based on the cost of the group. For example, if bubblegum is 2 packs for 20¢, then divide 20 by 2 to find out the unit price of each pack: 10¢.

1 burger patty costs _____.

A burger special with 2 burger buns, 3 slices of tomato, 3 lettuce leaves, and 2 burger patties costs _____.

32 pasta strands cost _____.

1 French fry costs _____.

3 chicken fingers cost _____.

1 cookie costs _____.

Division Grinding

When you divide numbers, the answer you get is the **quotient**.

To solve long division equations:

1. Place the number you're dividing by (the **divisor**) to the left of the number you're dividing it into (the **dividend**).

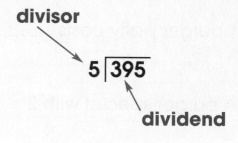

2. Figure out how many times the divisor goes into the largest possible place value in the dividend. Write your answer above that value in the quotient.

$$5\overline{)395}$$

$$\overset{7}{5\overline{)395}}$$

3. Multiply, then subtract, and bring down any amount still remaining in the quotient.

$$\begin{array}{r} 7 \\ 5\overline{)395} \\ 35 \\ \hline 45 \end{array}$$

4. Continue until there are no digits left to bring down

$$\begin{array}{r} 79 \leftarrow \textbf{quotient} \\ 5\overline{)395} \\ 35 \\ \hline 45 \end{array}$$

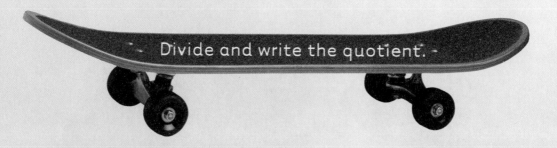

Divide and write the quotient.

$$4\overline{)64} \qquad\qquad 7\overline{)84}$$

3)69   6)78

7)98      2)824

9)171      8)432

4)656      5)230

A Division Riddle

Divide, and write the quotients.

$5\overline{)850}$ x $3\overline{)27}$ b $9\overline{)54}$ s $4\overline{)72}$ i $5\overline{)55}$ r $5\overline{)40}$ w

$2\overline{)86}$ y

$6\overline{)90}$ e

$8\overline{)48}$ s

$4\overline{)76}$ t

$2\overline{)48}$ a

$2\overline{)824}$ o

$9\overline{)171}$ t

$6\overline{)288}$ l

$3\overline{)954}$ u

$7\overline{)126}$ i

$4\overline{)324}$ h

$4\overline{)196}$ z

Use the letters next to the quotients above to answer the riddle below.

What do you get if you cross an artist with a police officer?

___   ___ ___ ___ ___ ___
24   9   11   318   6   81

___ ___ ___ ___   ___ ___ ___   ___ ___ ___
8   18   19   81   19   81   15   48   24   8

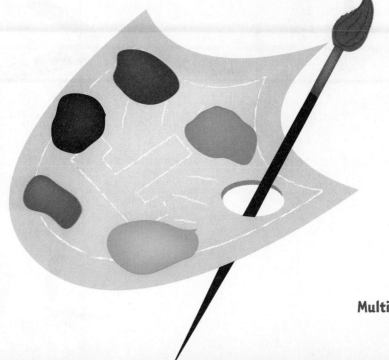

Math Juggling

Write the numbers in the balls that complete the equations. Choose from the numbers in the box. Hint: One single-digit number is used more than once.

200	8
5	9
16	12
180	14
99	2
4	

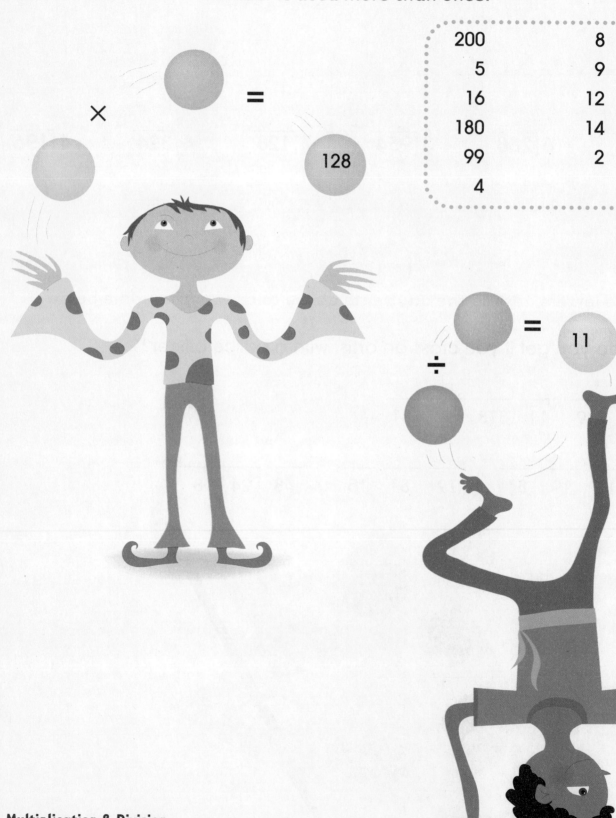

× ◯ = 128

◯ ÷ ◯ = 11

A Math Treasure Chest

Ahoy, mateys! See if you can find the missing numbers and symbols on this treasure trove of math!

	÷	4	=	4		10	×		=	500	100
×		×				×		÷			÷
6	×		÷	5	=	24		10	×	10	=	
=		÷		×		×		=		=	×
	÷	8	=	12			÷	5	=	50	25
		=		÷		=					=
10	×	10	×		=	60,000		75	÷		=	25
			=						×	
	÷	18	=	1		864			21	
×		÷			49		7	×	2	=	14
3	×	9	=	27		4			63		2
=		=		+		=					×
54	×		+	108	=	216		108	÷	9	=	
			=								=
810	÷	6	=			12	×		÷	4	=	24

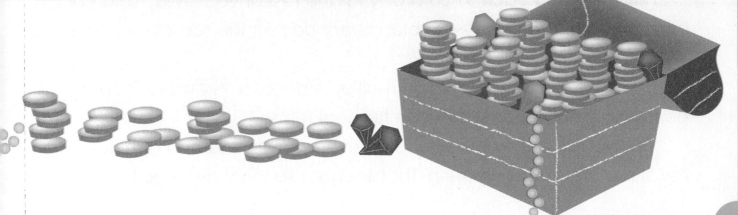

The Good-Deal Girls

Once upon a time in a faraway land, there lived a pair of twins, Penelope and Priscilla. The girls were very wise, but not very wealthy.

"Let's take a voyage around the world to see what we can learn and *earn*," said Priscilla.

"I'll pack sandwiches," said Penelope.

The twins set off. Before they had gone very far, they came upon an enchanted frog. The crown on his head and the fact that he was whistling were a dead giveaway.

"Hello, girls. Yes, indeed, I am an enchanted frog," said the frog. "You know the old story: handsome prince has evil spell cast on him and gets turned into a frog. There are two ways I can be released. The first is for a pretty young maiden, such as one of you two, to give me a kiss."

"Ugh!" said Penelope. "I don't think so. What's the other way?"

The frog was clearly disappointed. "Oh, well," he said. "We'll have to go with choice number 2. I must do a good turn for someone else and be released because of my own kindness. More work for me, but I am tired of life on a lily pad."

The frog hopped closer to the girls. "I know you're looking for a way to become wealthy," he said slyly. "I'll make you an offer."

"What's your offer?" asked Penelope, ever practical.

"I will offer you each $1.00 a day for the rest of your lives," said the frog. "Or I will give you 1¢ doubled every day for the rest of your lives. Which do you want?"

"Let's take $1.00 a day," said Priscilla. "A dollar is 99¢ more than a penny, so that sounds like the better deal to me."

"Yes, but the penny gets doubled every day," Penelope reminded her. "I like that doubling thing. That sounds like the way to go to me."

"Dollar!" said Priscilla.

"Doubling pennies!" said Penelope.

The twins kept arguing back and forth, round and round. They were arguing so loudly they didn't even notice when the frog threw up his webbed hands, shook his head, and hopped away. (Soon after, the frog met a maiden who did give him a kiss. He became a prince again, the two fell in love, got married, and lived happily ever after.)

As for Priscilla and Penelope, they learned some important lessons.

"Always figure out the math," said Priscilla.

"And keep your eye on those enchanted frogs," said Penelope. (Soon after, they met up with the frog-prince and got great jobs in his countinghouse, counting all his money. The twins saved their salaries wisely, eventually bought their own castle, and then they, too, lived happily ever after.)

THE END.

Use the information in the story to answer these questions.

If the girls had each gotten their wish, who would have had more money after 10 days: Priscilla or Penelope?

Why? _____

Which of the twins would have had more money after 12 days?

Why? _____

How much more money would one of the sisters have had than the other after 15 days?

Why? _____

If she didn't spend a cent of it, how many days would it have taken Priscilla

to get $1,000? _____ How about Penelope? _____

The Factor Face-Off

Take careful aim. Then see how many factors you can knock down with just one hit!

You Need
- a partner
- 15 counters for each player (beans, coins, or buttons will work; make sure each player gets a different color.)
- paper and pencil
- the game cards on this page

1. Each player takes a turn. Pick any number except 0. Write your number on the paper to keep track of the numbers you use.

2. Say your number out loud. Put a counter on all the factors of the number you called. When you can't cover any more factors, your turn is over. On your next turn, pick a different number.

3. The game is over when all of the factors have been covered. The player with the most factors covered wins.

7	5	1	20	8
22	15	9	30	24
12	21	25	3	4
	16	2	10	

7	5	1	20	8
22	15	9	30	24
12	21	25	3	4
	16	2	10	

Something to think about: Why do the rules say that you can't call 0?

There is no 0 on the board, so you wouldn't be able to place any counters on it if you called it out.

Multiplication & Division Answer Key

Note: Answers read across per page, except for pages 76–77.

74–75 Answers will vary.

76–77 10, 15, 20, 25; 8, 12, 16; 12, 18, 24, 30, 36; fish and chips; 6, 14, 28, 42, 9, 21, 35, 49, it splits; 16, 32, 48, 64, 24, 40, 56; a goblet; 18, 27, 36, 45, 54, 63, 72, 81; big hands

78–79 26, 12, 15, 33, 28, 6, 54, 88, 49, 25; answers will vary.

80–81 baboons/396/a tribe, kangaroos/4,368/a troop, toads/869/a knot, oysters/726/a bed, cattle/1,642/a drove, turkeys/1,728/a rafter, crows/3,450/a murder, parrots/387/a company, ponies/362/a string

82–83 71 + 1 = 1 + 71, 60 + 12 = 12 + 60, 12 x 6 = 6 x 12, 9 x 8 = 8 x 9, 36 x 2 = 2 x 36, 17 + 55 = 55 + 17, 69 + 3 = 3 + 69, 45 + 27 = 27 + 45, 24 x 3 = 3 x 24, 18 x 4 = 4 x 18, 48 + 24 = 24 + 48, 1 x 72 = 72 x 1; d, i, j, e, a, b, f, k, g, c, l, h; all sums or products equal 72.

84–85 6 x 2 = 12, 7 x 8 = 56, 10 x 10 = 100, (4 x 4) + (2 x 10) = 16 + 20 = 36, (3 x 8) + (4 x 6) = 24 + 24 = 48, (10 x 4) + (5 x 2) + (6 x 10) = 40 + 10 + 60 = 110, (5 x 4) + (12 x 2) = 20 + 24 = 44; (177 x 2 x 3) = (354 x 3) = 1,062 + (3 x 4) + (3 x 6) + (3 x 10) = 1,062 + 12 + 18 + 30 = 1,122

86–87 walrus: 18, elephant: 6, otter: 36, baleen whale: 0, sea otter: 32, cat: 30, jackrabbit: 28, porcupine: 20, mouse: 16, pig: 44, skunk: 34, squirrel: 22, opossum: 50, polar bear: 42, raccoon: 40

88–89 280, 100 x 365 = 36,500, 10,000 x 365 = 3,650,000, 50 x 365 = 18,250, 70 x 24 = 1,680, 40 x 365 = 14,600, 360,000 x 24 = 8,640,000

90–91 **Delaware:** 110, **Maine:** 90, **Connecticut:** 224, **Ontario:** 192, **North Carolina:** 133, **Missouri:** 117, **Minnesota:** 78, **Alaska:** 272, **New Mexico:** 126, **New Jersey:** 228

92–93 8 ÷ 2 = 4, 12 ÷ 4 = 3, 15 ÷ 5 = 3, 21 ÷ 7 = 3, 16 ÷ 4 = 4; 2, 7, 4, 4, 5

94–95 r. 5 x 6 ≠ 25, e. 48 ÷ 3 = 16, r. 87 ÷ 7 ≠ 12, h. 15 x 3 ≠ 39, r. 8 x 9 = 72, r. 66 ÷ 4 ≠ 14, b. 448 ÷ 56 = 8, r. 103 x 9 ≠ 936, e. 493 ÷ 32 ≠ 6; a. 210 x 4 = 840, r. 138 ÷ 6 = 23, b. 12 x 11 = 132; barber

96–97 1, 2, 3, 4, 5, 6, 7, 8, 9, 10, 11, 12, 13, 14, 15, 16, 17, 18, 19, 20

98–99 10 ÷ 2 = 5, 8 ÷ 2 = 4, 250 ÷ 5 = 50, 8 x 3 = 24 ÷ 2 = 12, 250 x 2 = 500 ÷ 10 = 50, 11,000 ÷ 10 = 1,100, 11,100 ÷ 2 = 5,500, 11,000 ÷ 8 = 1,375, 11,000 ÷ 5 = 2,200, 11,000 ÷ 250 = 44

100–101 72

102–103 24, 37, 36, 60, 63, 48, 94

104–105 See below; 11

106–107 The final answers are always: 6, 4, 5, 3, 2, 6, 2, the number you started with.

108–109 Answers will vary.

110–111 300, 180, 0, 5, 80; see below.

112–113 20, 51, 12, 5, 4

114–115 50¢, 96¢, 11¢, $2.67, $2.08, 20¢

116–117 16, 12, 23, 13, 14, 412, 19, 54, 164, 46

118–119 x. 170, b. 9, s. 6, i. 18, r. 11, w. 8, y. 43, e. 15, s. 6, t. 19, a. 24, o. 412, t. 19, l. 48, u. 318, i. 18, h. 81, z. 49; a brush with the law

120–121 16 x 8, 99 ÷ 9, 180 ÷ 2, 12 x 5, 200 ÷ 5, 14 x 4

122–123 See below.

124–125 Priscilla, 10 x $1 = $10 (Penelope would have 1¢ x 2 = 2¢ x 2 = 4¢ x 2 = 8¢ x 2 = 16¢ x 2 = 32¢ x 2 = 64¢ x 2 = $1.28 x 2 = $2.56 x 2 = $5.12); Penelope, $5.12 x 2 = $10.24 x 2 = $20.48 (Priscilla would have 12 x $1 = $12); Penelope would have had $148.84 more than Priscilla. (Penelope would have had $163.84 and Priscilla would have had $15.); Priscilla= 1,000 days, Penelope=18 days. (On the 18th day, she would have had $1,310.72.)

104–105

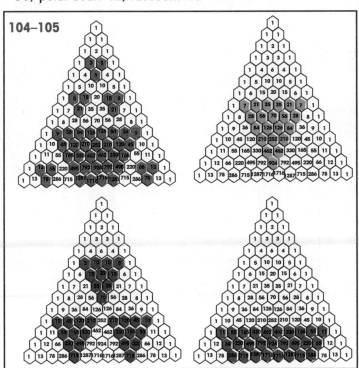

110–111

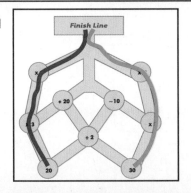

122–123

16	÷	4	=	4		10	×	50	=	500		100
×		×				x		÷		÷		÷
6	×	20	÷	5	=	24		10	×	10	=	100
=		÷		×		×		=		=		×
96	÷	8	=	12		250	÷	5	=	50		25
		=		÷		=						=
10	×	10	×	600	=	60,000		75	÷	3	=	25
				=						×		
18	÷	18	=	1		864			21			
×		÷			49	÷	7	×	2	=	14	
3	×	9	=	27	4				63			2
=		=		+				=				×
54	×	2	+	108	=	216		108	÷	9	=	12
		=						=				=
810	÷	6	=	135		12	×	8	÷	4	=	24

Halve Fun!

How many ways can you divide a square in half? Here are two ways:

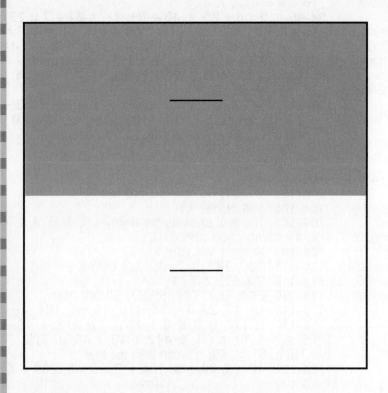

Write the fraction for one-half on the shaded side of each square. What fraction would the unshaded side be? Write it.

Color in the unshaded side on both squares. What do you have now?

? + ? = 1 whole

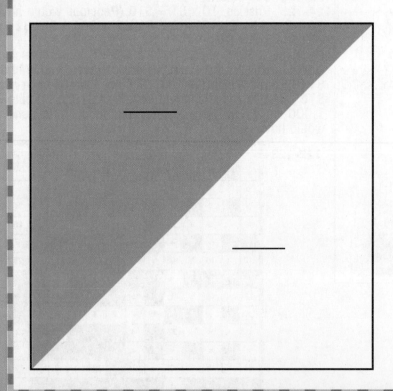

Look at all the squares below. See how many ways you can
find to divide the squares in half. Don't forget: The small
squares themselves form bigger squares, which can be divided!

You're a Grand Old Fraction . . .

Draw a line from each country to its flag. The fractions shown in color will give you a clue. Hint: You will have to write the fractions for three countries. Look at the color clue, find the matching flag, and write the fraction.

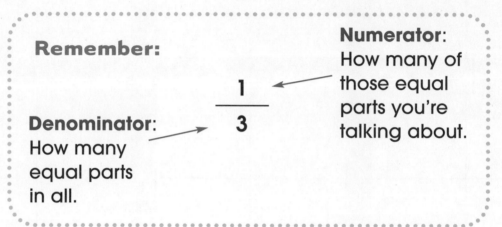

Remember:

Numerator: How many of those equal parts you're talking about.

$$\frac{1}{3}$$

Denominator: How many equal parts in all.

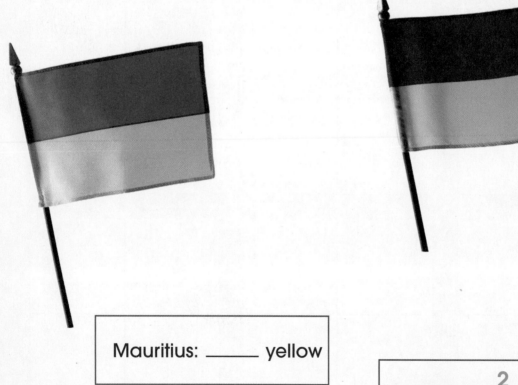

Mauritius: _____ yellow

Nigeria: $\dfrac{2}{3}$ green

Ethiopia: $\dfrac{1}{3}$ green

Ukraine: _____ yellow

Thailand: $\dfrac{2}{6}$ blue

Monaco: _____ white

How Low Can You Go?

Some fractions can be written in two ways. For example, $\frac{5}{10} = \frac{1}{2}$.

Writing a fraction in this way is called reducing a fraction to its lowest term.

To reduce a fraction to its lowest terms

1. Find the greatest number that will divide evenly into both the numerator and denominator. In $\frac{5}{10}$, 5 is the greatest number that will divide into both parts of the fraction evenly.

2. Divide both parts. $\frac{5 \ (\div 5)}{10 \ (\div 5)} = \frac{1}{2}$

Reduce the fractions below. Write each answer in the other mitten.

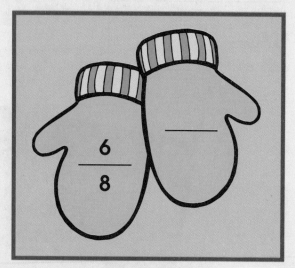

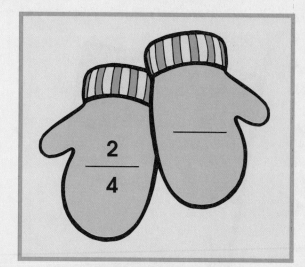

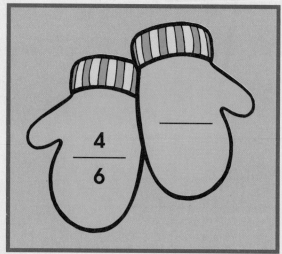

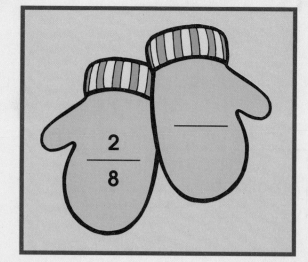

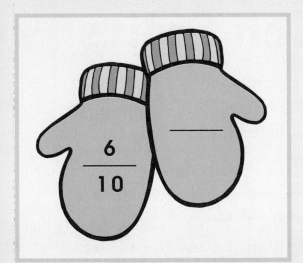

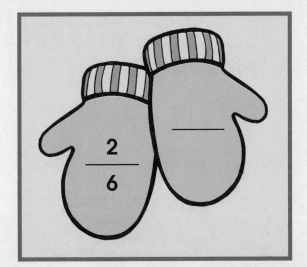

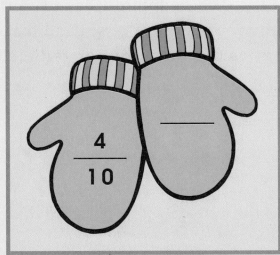

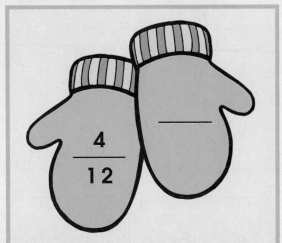

How many ways can you write $\dfrac{1}{2}$? Fill in the numerators.

$\dfrac{\quad}{4}$ $\dfrac{\quad}{6}$ $\dfrac{\quad}{8}$ $\dfrac{\quad}{10}$ $\dfrac{\quad}{12}$

How many ways can you write $\dfrac{1}{5}$? Fill in the numerators.

$\dfrac{\quad}{10}$ $\dfrac{\quad}{20}$ $\dfrac{\quad}{30}$ $\dfrac{\quad}{40}$ $\dfrac{\quad}{50}$

Sandwich Splits

Maria's mom made sandwiches and divided them. Maria and her friends are going to share the sandwich parts.

Read the directions below each sandwich. Color each friend's share a different color. Write the two fractions that describe what each friend gets. Hint: The denominator of the first fraction describes the total number of parts. The second fraction describes the colors you used and is the first fraction reduced.

Share this sandwich among 4 friends.

Each friend gets ———, or ———,
             8   4

of the sandwich. Remember: the first denominator is the number of sandwich pieces. The second denominator is the number of colors you used.

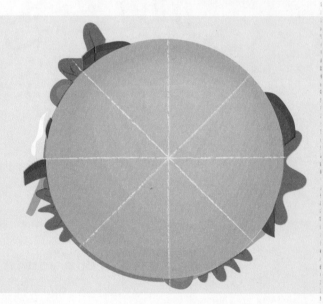

Share this sandwich among 2 friends.

Each friend gets ———, or ———,
of the sandwich.

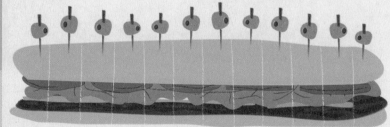

Share this sandwich among 5 friends.

Each friend gets _____ , or _____ , of the sandwich.

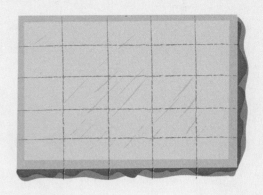

Share this sandwich among 6 friends.

Each friend gets _____ , or _____ , of the sandwich.

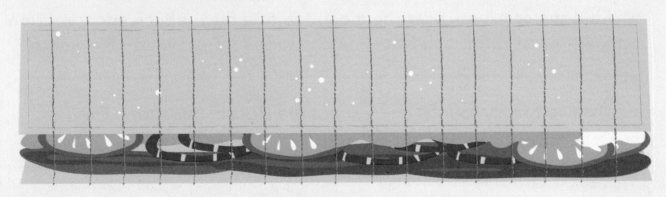

Share these mini-sandwiches among 6 friends.

Each friend gets _____ , or _____ , of the total number of mini-sandwiches.

Sky-High Fractions

Why did the cow jump over the moon? To find out, reduce each fraction to its lowest term, and write the answer as a fraction and in words.

Twelve twenty-fourths ($\frac{12}{24}$) of the stars in this scene are red.

What fraction is that in lowest terms? _____

___ ___ ___ - ___ ___ ___ ___
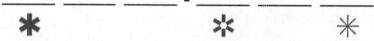

What fraction of stars in the scene are yellow? _____

What fraction is that in lowest terms? _____

___ ___ ___- ___ ___ ___ ___ ___ ___

What fraction of stars in the scene are five-pointed? _____

What fraction is that in lowest terms? _____

___ ___ ___ ___- ___ ___ ___ ___ ___ ___ ___

What fraction of the stars making up the

Big Dipper are yellow and five-pointed? _____

___ ___ ___ ___ ___-
                    ✴

___ ___ ___ ___ ___ ___ ___ ___
                    ✦

What fraction of the red stars are five-pointed? _____

What fraction is that in lowest terms? _____

___ ___ ___ ___-___ ___ ___ ___ ___
                              ✴ ✴

Find the symbols, and write the letters from your answers to solve the riddle.

___ ___ ___ ___ ___ ___
✴ ✴ ✴ ✴ ✴ ✴

___ ___ ___ ___ ___
☆ ✴ ✴ ✴ ✴

___ ___ ___ ___ ___ ___ ___ ___ ___ ___ ___
✴ ✴ ✴ ✴ ✴ ✴ ✴ ✴ ✴ ✴

Ice-Cold Fractions

Color in each cup to show how much of it will be filled by the recipe.
Remember: You add only the numerators to get the answer.
Then, wherever possible, reduce the sum of the fractions
to the lowest common denominator.

$\dfrac{1}{4}$ cup grapefruit juice + $\dfrac{1}{4}$ cup cherry juice

Sweet and Sour Sipper

$$\underline{\quad\quad}$$

$\dfrac{2}{4}$ cup apple juice + $\dfrac{1}{4}$ cup pineapple juice

Hawaiian Apple

_____

$\dfrac{1}{6}$ cup orange juice + $\dfrac{3}{6}$ cup fruit punch

A Punch of Orange

_____

$\dfrac{1}{3}$ cup mango nectar + $\dfrac{1}{3}$ cup tomato juice

Tomango Juice

_____

$\dfrac{2}{8}$ cup orange juice + $\dfrac{1}{8}$ cup ruby-red grapefruit juice

Ruby-Red OJ

_____

$\dfrac{3}{4}$ cup grape juice + $\dfrac{1}{4}$ cup cherry juice

Grape Balls of Cherry Juice

_____

Hint: Mix up these cool concoctions yourself. Turn them into freeze pops. Pour the mixtures into ice-cube trays, and chill in the freezer for about 30 minutes. Add a Popsicle stick to each one, and freeze until hard.

Any Way You Slice It

When Tiny McGee entered the Pottstown Pie-Eating Contest, he didn't realize he'd have to put together the pies himself! Help him by drawing lines to connect the parts of the pies that together create a whole pie.

Write a fraction addition equation for each kind of pie parts you put together.

_____

_____

_____

_____

How many whole pies will Tiny eat if he eats all of the pies on the table?

_____

Will there be any partial pies left over for Tiny to eat after he eats all the whole pies he can put together? If so, what fraction of a whole pie will that be?

_____

Now figure out how many whole and partial pies
each of these contestants ate.

Apple-Pie Annie

Dixie Jane

Chad N. Chew

Potbelly Pete

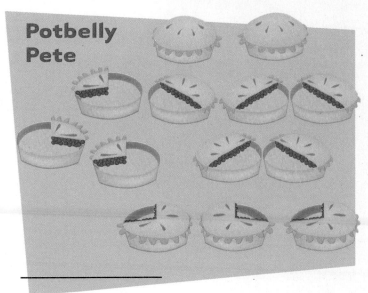

Which of these pie eaters ate the most
and won the contest?

_____

Sneaky Pizzas

Someone is sneaking off with pizza slices! Write a subtraction equation to describe what fraction of the slices are missing from each pizza. The first one has been done for you. Hint: Reduce your answer to the lowest terms possible

$$\frac{8}{8} - \frac{5}{8} = \frac{3}{8}$$

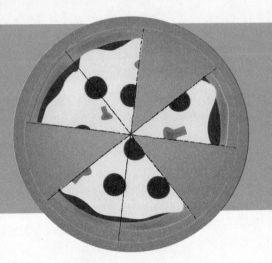

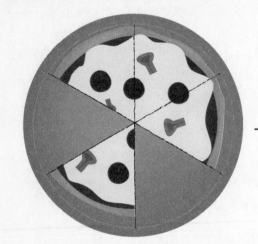

$$\underline{\hphantom{8}} - \underline{\hphantom{8}} = \underline{\hphantom{8}}$$

$$\underline{\hphantom{8}} - \underline{\hphantom{8}} = \underline{\hphantom{8}}$$

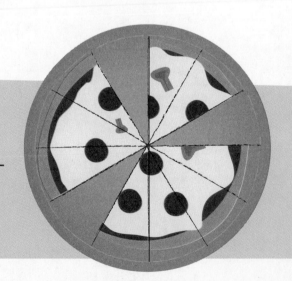

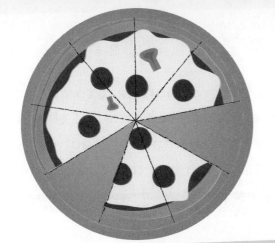

$$\frac{}{} - \frac{}{} = \frac{}{}$$

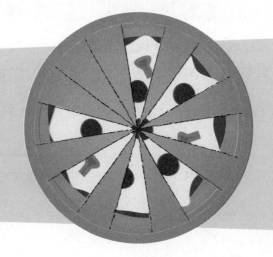

$$\frac{}{} - \frac{}{} = \frac{}{}$$

$$\frac{}{} - \frac{}{} = \frac{}{}$$

Now draw lines on the pizzas to show these equations.
Color in the remaining slices.

$$\frac{5}{5} - \frac{4}{5}$$ $$\frac{12}{12} - \frac{6}{12}$$

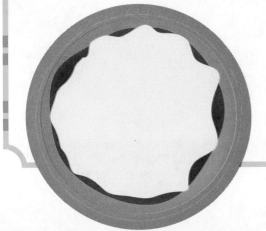

Fractured Fractions

Color in the circle sections to match the fraction next to each one. Then put the fractions in order to show the correct order of the cartoon panels. Start by writing 1 in the box with the smallest fraction. Go up to 7, the largest fraction. Hint: Look in the box if you need help.

Ordering Fractions

If two fractions have the same denominator, the fraction with the greater numerator is larger. For example, $\dfrac{3}{5} > \dfrac{2}{5}$.

If two fractions have the same numerator, the fraction with the lesser denominator is larger. For example, $\dfrac{1}{3} > \dfrac{1}{5}$.

If two fractions have different numerators and denominators, rename one or both fractions so their denominators are the same. Then compare numerators. $\dfrac{1}{2} \; (= \dfrac{2}{4}) < \dfrac{3}{4}$

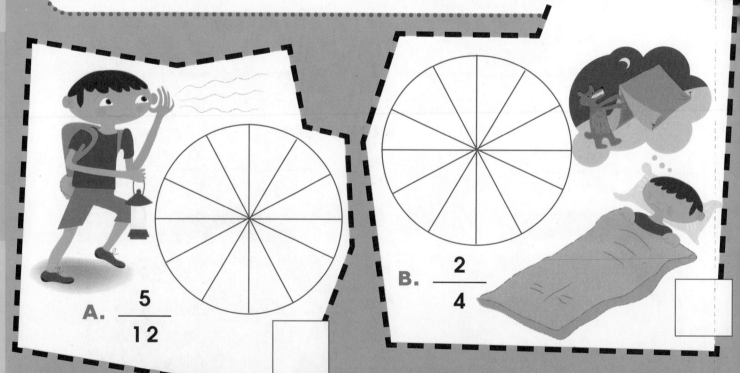

A. $\dfrac{5}{12}$

B. $\dfrac{2}{4}$

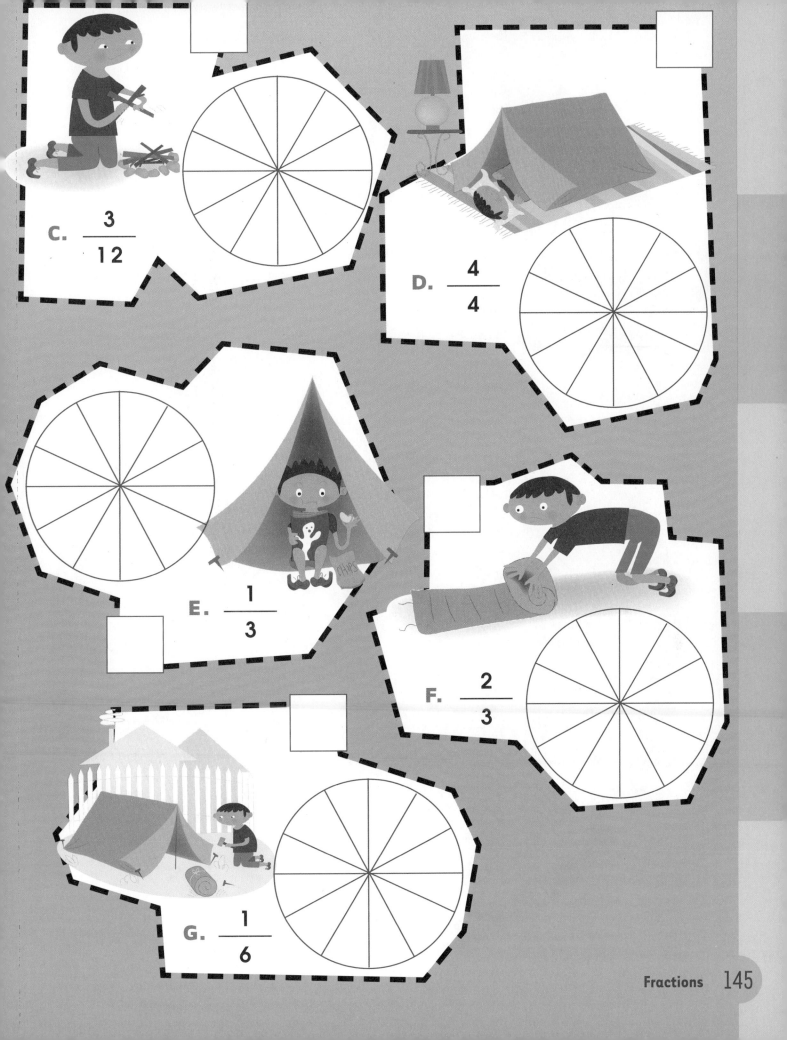

C. $\dfrac{3}{12}$

D. $\dfrac{4}{4}$

E. $\dfrac{1}{3}$

F. $\dfrac{2}{3}$

G. $\dfrac{1}{6}$

Wheel of Fractions

Solve each fraction addition or subtraction equation.

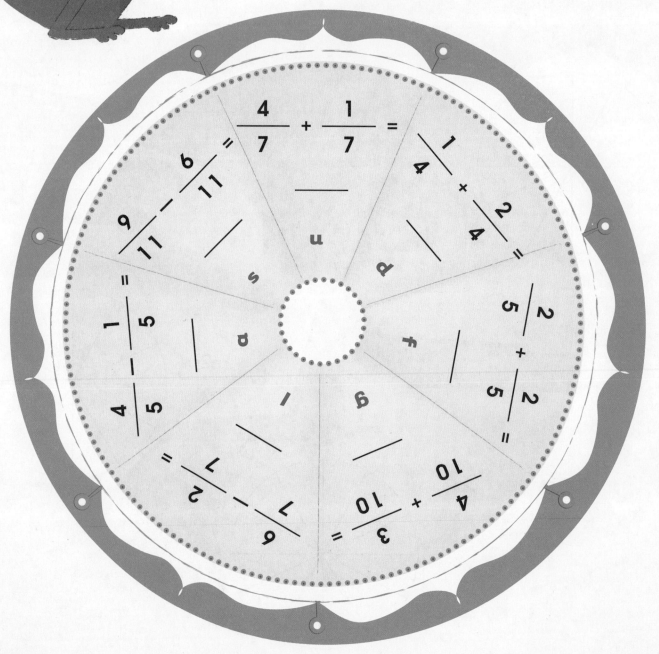

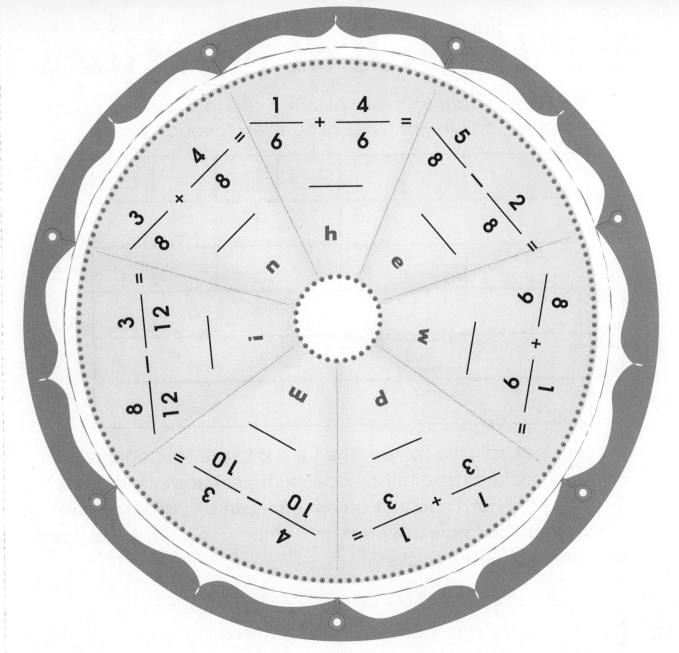

Use the letters next to your answers above to solve the riddle below.

Why did the watchdog spin around and around and around?

$\dfrac{5}{6}$ $\dfrac{3}{8}$ $\dfrac{7}{9}$ $\dfrac{3}{5}$ $\dfrac{3}{11}$

$\dfrac{7}{9}$ $\dfrac{5}{12}$ $\dfrac{7}{8}$ $\dfrac{3}{4}$ $\dfrac{5}{12}$ $\dfrac{7}{8}$ $\dfrac{7}{10}$

$\dfrac{5}{6}$ $\dfrac{5}{12}$ $\dfrac{1}{10}$ $\dfrac{3}{11}$ $\dfrac{3}{8}$ $\dfrac{4}{7}$ $\dfrac{4}{5}$ $\dfrac{5}{7}$ $\dfrac{2}{3}$

Build a Wall of Fractions

1. On your turn, spin the spinner. The idea is to put your counters on as many bricks as possible on each turn. For example, if you spin $\frac{5}{6}$, you could put 5 counters on the one-sixth bricks. But a better move would be to put counters on 4 of the one-eighth bricks and on 2 of the one-sixth bricks:

$$\frac{1}{8} + \frac{1}{8} + \frac{1}{8} + \frac{1}{8} + \frac{1}{6} + \frac{1}{6} = \frac{5}{6}.$$

2. The game ends when there is a counter on each brick. The player with the most bricks wins.

Use the pencil and paper clip to make an "arrow" for the spinner. Flick the paper clip. It will spin around the pencil point.

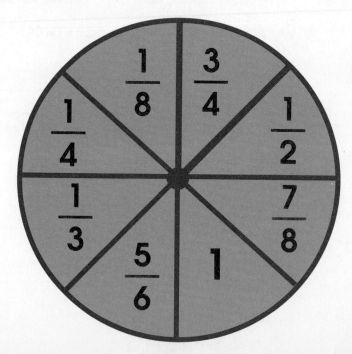

Fractions Answer Key

Note: Answers read across, per page.

128–129 $\frac{1}{2}$, $\frac{1}{2}$, $\frac{1}{2}$, $\frac{1}{2}$; answers will vary.

130–131 Draw lines as directed; **Monaco:** $\frac{1}{2}$, **Ukraine:** $\frac{1}{2}$, **Mauritius:** $\frac{1}{4}$

132–133 $\frac{3}{4}$, $\frac{1}{2}$, $\frac{2}{3}$, $\frac{1}{4}$, $\frac{3}{5}$, $\frac{1}{3}$, $\frac{2}{5}$, $\frac{1}{3}$; 2, 3, 4, 5, 6; 2, 4, 6, 8, 10

134–135 $\frac{2}{8}$, $\frac{1}{4}$; $\frac{6}{12}$, $\frac{1}{2}$; $\frac{5}{25}$, $\frac{1}{5}$; $\frac{3}{18}$, $\frac{1}{6}$; $\frac{2}{12}$, $\frac{1}{6}$

136–137 $\frac{1}{2}$, one-half; $\frac{6}{24}$, $\frac{1}{4}$, one-fourth, $\frac{20}{24}$, five-sixths; $\frac{3}{7}$, three-sevenths;

$\frac{8}{12}$, $\frac{2}{3}$, two-thirds; for the udder thrill of it

138–139 Color one-half, $\frac{1}{2}$; color three-quarters, $\frac{3}{4}$; color four-sixths, $\frac{2}{3}$,

color two-thirds, $\frac{2}{3}$; color three-eighths, $\frac{3}{8}$; color $\frac{4}{4}$, 1

140–141 $\frac{1}{2} + \frac{1}{2} = 1$; $\frac{1}{4} + \frac{3}{4} = 1$; $\frac{3}{4} + \frac{1}{4} = 1$; 10, $\frac{3}{4}$; 7, 8, $9\frac{1}{2}$, $7\frac{1}{2}$; Tiny McGee

142–143 $\frac{6}{6} - \frac{4}{6} = \frac{2}{6} = \frac{1}{3}$, $\frac{12}{12} - \frac{9}{12} = \frac{3}{12} = \frac{1}{4}$, $\frac{9}{9} - \frac{7}{9} = \frac{2}{9}$,

$\frac{16}{16} - \frac{7}{16} = \frac{9}{16}$, $\frac{10}{10} - \frac{5}{10} = \frac{5}{10} = \frac{1}{2}$; pizza should be divided into fifths, one fifth colored;

pizza should be divided into twelfths, one-half colored

144–145 A. 4, B. 5. C. 2, D. 7, E. 3, F. 6, G. 1

146–147 u $\frac{5}{7}$, d $\frac{3}{4}$, f $\frac{4}{5}$, g $\frac{7}{10}$, l $\frac{4}{7}$, a $\frac{3}{5}$, s $\frac{3}{11}$; h $\frac{5}{6}$, e $\frac{3}{8}$, w $\frac{7}{9}$, p $\frac{2}{3}$,

m $\frac{1}{10}$, i $\frac{5}{12}$, n $\frac{7}{8}$; he was winding himself up

1
2
3
4
5
6
7
8

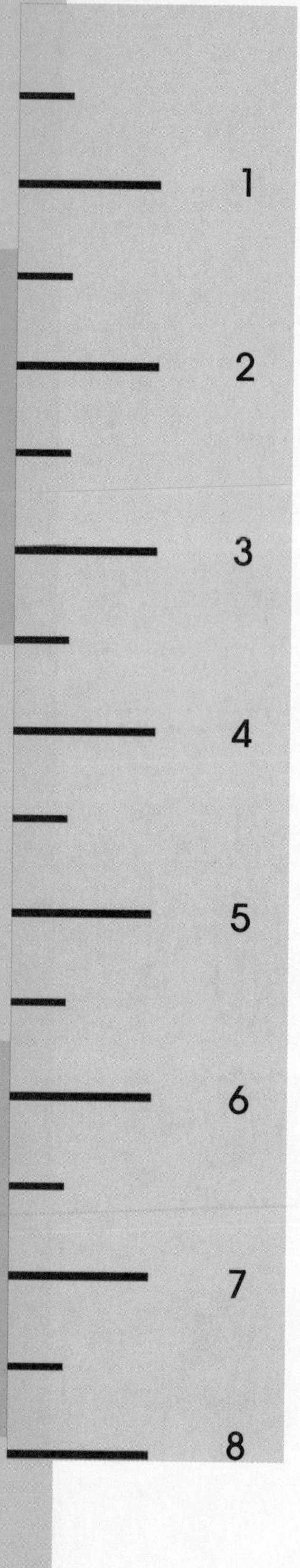

Drawing on Measurement

Draw a picture of each art tool to the size specified. Hint: Some sizes are standard; some are metric measurements. The rulers along the sides of the page will help you estimate. Then measure each item carefully to see how close you came!

crayon: 4 inches long

eraser: 5 centimeters long

paintbrush: $17\frac{1}{2}$ centimeters long

Metric Ruler (centimeters)

1
2
3
4
5
6
7
8
9
10
11
12
13
14
15
16
17
18
19
20

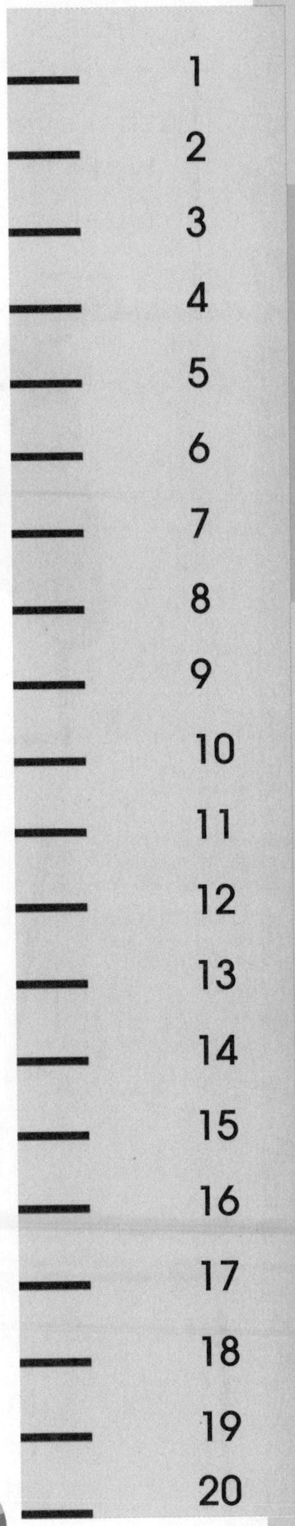

pencil:
$7\frac{1}{2}$ inches long

pen: 15 centimeters long

safety scissors:
5 inches long

Which measurements are standard? ______________

Which measurements are metric? ______________

Going to Great Lengths

There's more than one way to describe the average size of these incredible creatures. Write the measurements. The clues in the box will help you.

Atlas Moth, the world's largest moth
Wingspan: 1 foot

That's the same as _____ inches.

Whale Shark, the world's biggest fish
Average length: 30 feet

That's the same as _____ inches, or _____ yards.

Komodo Dragon,
the world's largest lizard
Length: up to 10 feet

It would take _____ Komodo dragons to equal the length of 1 whale shark.

Giraffe,
the world's tallest land mammal
Height: 18 feet.

That's the same as _____ inches, or _____ yards.

Bee Hummingbird,
the world's smallest bird

Size: $2\frac{1}{2}$ inches from the tip

of its bill to the end of its tail

Dwarf Pygmy Goby,
the world's smallest fish

Length: $\frac{1}{2}$ inch

Stick Insect, the world's longest insect
Length: 1 foot, 10 inches

That's the same as _____ inches.

It would take _____ dwarf pygmy goby fish

to equal the size of 1 bee hummingbird.

It would take _____ dwarf pygmy goby fish

to equal the length of 1 whale shark.

The Longest Lace

Ralph has a broken shoelace. Help him replace it with the longest one from this bunch on his floor. How long do you think each shoelace is? Write your estimates below.

Now measure each shoelace one at a time. Write your answers under "Actual." (Use standard measurements.) Then compare the measurements with your estimates. Finally, write the shoelace measurements as metric measurements. Hint: 1 inch = about $2\frac{1}{2}$ centimeters

Shoelace	Estimated Length	Actual Length	Metric Measurement
A	_____	_____	_____
B	_____	_____	_____
C	_____	_____	_____
D	_____	_____	_____
E	_____	_____	_____

Which shoelace is the longest? _____

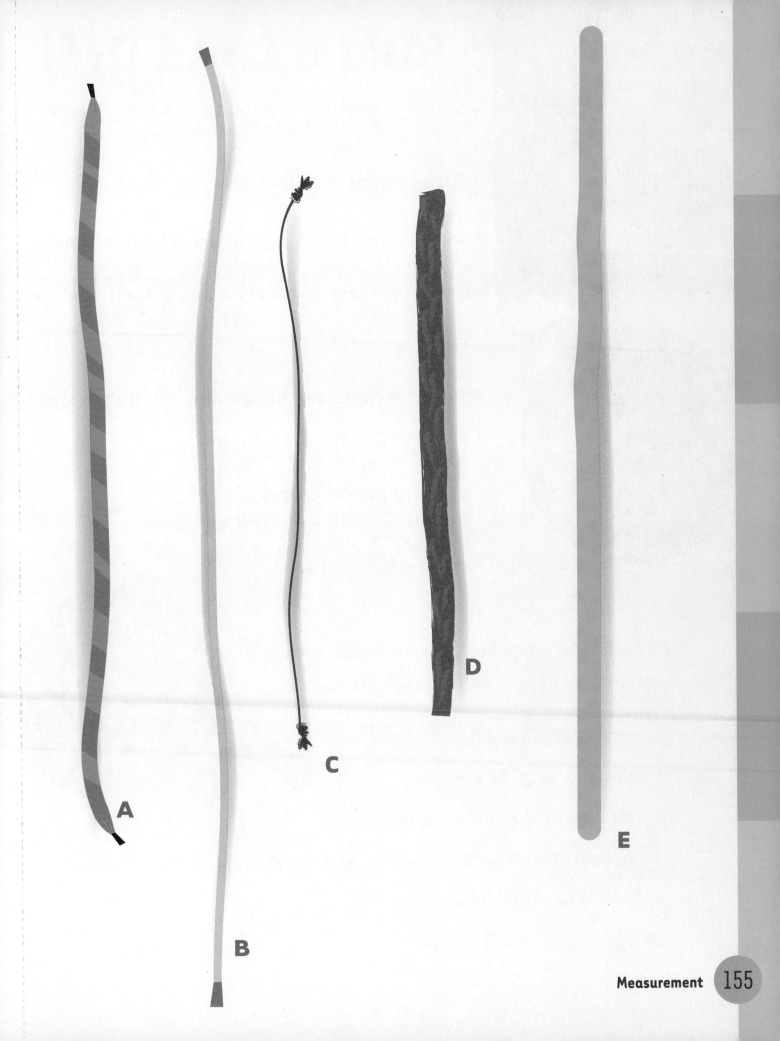

A

B

C

D

E

Take a Load Off!

Can you help this hiker lighten his camping load?
The clues in the box will help you

Customary Weights

16 ounces = 1 pound
This means that 20 ounces = 1 pound, 4 ounces

1. Add up the weight of these items. What's the total?

_____ ounces, or _____ pound

cooking pot: 8 ounces
map and compass: 3 ounces
flashlight: 3 ounces
batteries: 2 ounces

2. Rewrite the weight of each of these items in pounds or in pounds and ounces.

first-aid kit: 16 ounces _____

sleeping bag: 32 ounces _____

change of clothes: 24 ounces _____

stove, matches, and jackknife: 30 ounces _____

food and water: 34 ounces _____

3. What's the total weight of all the items in 1 and 2?

_____ ounces, or _____ pounds, _____ ounces

- -

4. What would the new weight be if a camper left the change of clothes at home?

_____ ounces, or _____ pounds

- -

5. What would the new weight be if a camper left the change of clothes and the cooking pot at home?

_____ ounces, or _____ pounds, _____ ounces

- -

6. Suppose a camper left behind the change of clothes and the cooking pot, but still wanted to carry only 5 pounds. What other items could be left behind? _____

Clutter in the Kitchen!

Help Fred combine the containers in his refrigerator that have the same kinds of liquids in them. The clues in the box will help you.

Liquid Measures
2 cups = 1 pint
2 pints = 1 quart
2 quarts = 1 half gallon
4 quarts = 1 gallon

LIQUID LUNCH ONE CUP

LIQUID LUNCH ONE CUP

LEMONY LIMEADE one pint

LEMONY LIMEADE one cup

LEMONY LIMEADE one cup

SI SI SI SIP O' SC SC SC SODA on on on one pint

SLIPPERY SALAD DRESSING

SLIPPERY SALAD DRESSING

ONE PINT

Write the steps in equations to show what size container Fred will need to combine these liquids. The first one is done for you.

Liquid Lunch $\underline{\text{1 cup + 1 cup =}}$

$\underline{\text{2 cups = 1 pint}}$

_____

Sip o' Soda _____

_____

_____

Lemony Limeade _____

_____

_____

Best Broth _____

_____

_____

Slippery Salad Dressing _____

_____

_____

SLIPPERY SALAD DRESSING

ONE QUART

BEST BROTH

1/2 gallon

BEST BROTH

one quart

BEST BROTH

one pint

BEST BROTH

one pint

Measure Your Metric Know-How

Remember:
To measure **distance**, use **meters**.
A baseball bat is about 1 meter long.
To measure things smaller than a basic unit, add these prefixes:
centi- = 1/100 of the basic unit. Example: **centi**meter
deci- = 1/10 of the basic unit. Example: **deci**meter

To measure **liquid volume**, use **liters**. There is about 1 liter of hot chocolate in 4 mugs.

To measure **weight**, use **grams**. A dollar bill weighs 1 gram. To measure things larger than a basic unit, add this prefix: kilo- = 1,000. Example: **kilo**gram

Use the words from the box to describe the measurement taking place in each scene. Write the correct measuring word on the line.

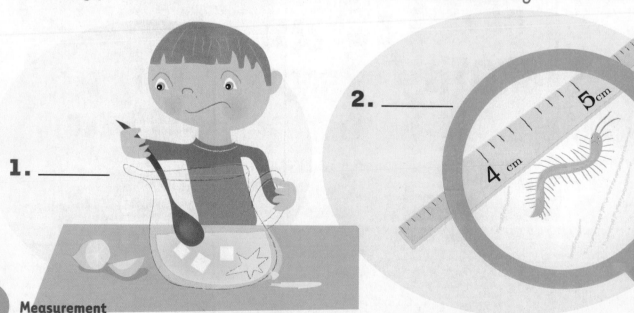

1. _____

2. _____

3. _____

4. _____

5. _____

6. _____

Chilling Riddles

Temperature is measured in Fahrenheit degrees. These numbers appear, with °F on the left side of the thermometer.

The metric measurement for degrees is Celsius. These numbers appear, with °C on the right side of the thermometer.

F

a 110
100
l 91
90
80
u 70
60
50
g 45
o 40
30
e 20
10
h 0
10
20

C

40 **o**
35 **y**
30
20 **s**
15 **k**
10
0 **f**
10
20 **t**
30

Use the degrees on the thermometer and the letters next to them to solve these spooky riddles. Hint: Some readings are given in degrees Fahrenheit (°F). Others are given in degrees Celsius (°C).

What do ghosts wear when they go out in the snow?

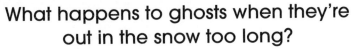

_____	_____	_____	_____	_____	-
45°F	0°F	40°C	70°F	91°F	

_____	_____	_____	_____	_____
40°C	20°C	0°F	20°F	20°C

What happens to ghosts when they're out in the snow too long?

_____	_____	_____	_____		_____	_____	_____
–20°C	0°F	20°F	35°C		45°F	20°F	–20°C

_____	_____	_____	_____	_____
0°C	91°F	110°F	15°C	35°C

Use the thermometer to answer these questions.

As the numbers on the thermometer go higher, should you wear more or fewer clothes when you go outside? _____

Would a snowman melt at 30°C or 30°F? _____

If a friend says, "It's 20 degrees, let's go outside and ice-skate," would your friend be talking about Celsius or Fahrenheit temperature?

_____

Measurement Search

Use these clues to fill in the missing math words.

There are 12 inches in 1 ___ ___ ___ ___.

An instrument used to measure time is a ___ ___ ___ ___ ___.

Meters, inches, feet, and yards are all units used to measure ___ ___ ___ ___ ___ ___.

A common 12-inch measuring tool is a ___ ___ ___ ___ ___.

There are 24 hours in one ___ ___ ___.

There are 60 minutes in one ___ ___ ___ ___ .

There are 365 days in one ___ ___ ___ ___.

A paperclip weighs about one ___ ___ ___ ___.

An instrument used to weigh something is a ___ ___ ___ ___ ___.

An instrument used to measure temperature is a ___ ___ ___ ___ ___ ___ ___ ___ ___ ___ ___.

There are 3 teaspoons in 1 ___ ___ ___ ___ ___ ___ ___.

There are 2 pints in 1 ___ ___ ___ ___ ___.

There are 16 ounces in 1 ___ ___ ___ ___ ___.

The metric measurement equal to $\frac{1}{1,000}$ meter is a ___ ___ ___ ___ ___ ___ ___ ___ ___ ___.

There are 60 seconds in 1 ___ ___ ___ ___ ___ ___.

A unit of measurement equal to $\frac{1}{12}$ of a foot is an ___ ___ ___ ___.

December is the twelfth ___ ___ ___ ___ ___ of the year.

There are 16 fluid ounces in 1 ___ ___ ___ ___.

The metric measurement equal to $\frac{1}{100}$ meter is

a ___ ___ ___ ___ ___ ___ ___ ___ ___ ___.

There are 4 quarts in 1 ___ ___ ___ ___ ___.

There are 3 feet, or 36 inches, in 1 ___ ___ ___ ___.

There are 10 years in 1 ___ ___ ___ ___ ___.

There are 5,280 feet in 1 ___ ___ ___ ___.

According to an old expression, "an ___ ___ ___ ___ ___ of prevention is worth a pound of cure."

Find the words you wrote above in the word puzzle. Words appear down, up, across, backward, and diagonally.

s	o	g	h	e	c	m	a	r	g	m	d
e	y	a	r	d	a	r	e	l	u	r	e
n	a	l	m	c	e	u	s	u	e	e	c
o	d	l	o	e	c	o	r	t	e	t	a
o	m	o	n	n	n	h	e	h	o	e	d
p	i	n	t	t	u	m	w	q	d	m	e
s	l	l	h	i	o	r	u	i	n	i	l
e	e	o	n	m	a	a	g	n	u	l	a
l	s	h	r	e	r	e	k	c	o	l	c
b	s	e	y	t	o	o	f	h	p	i	s
a	h	l	l	e	n	g	t	h	e	m	p
t	m	a	g	r	m	i	n	u	t	e	t

What's My Measurement?

Measure your estimation skills.

You Need • a partner • a ruler, tape measure, and/or meter stick • a kitchen or bathroom scale • the chart below

1. Decide if you'll play this game with standard units or metric units. (The kind of measuring tool and scale you have may make the decision for you!)
2. Write your estimates of each item's measurement on the chart.
3. Use the measurement tools to find the actual measurement of each item.
4. Score 1 point for each estimate you make that is closer than anyone else's. (If there's a tie on any measurement, you each score 1 point.)
5. The player with the most points after all the items have been measured wins.

	Player 1	Player 2	Actual Measurement
Lengths			
your thumb			
a fork			
a bicycle			
Widths			
your hand, fingers spread apart			
an open book			
a TV set			
Weights			
a bunch of bananas			
a pair of shoes			
a bag of marbles			

Play again, using whichever measuring units you didn't use the first time. Or make your own chart, and play with different items.

Measurement Answer Key

Note: Answers read across, per page.

150–151 Drawings should be to the specified sizes; **standard**: inches (crayon, pencil, safety scissors); **metric**: centimeters (eraser, paintbrush, pen)

152–153 12, 360, 10; 3, 216, 6; 22, 720, 5

154–155 A, 8 in./20 cm; B, 10 in./30 cm; C, $6\frac{1}{2}$ in./$16\frac{1}{4}$ cm; D, 5 in./$12\frac{1}{2}$ cm; E. $8\frac{1}{2}$ in./$21\frac{1}{4}$ cm

156–157 1. 16, 1, 2. 1 pound, 2 pounds; 1 pound, 8 ounces; 1 pound, 14 ounces; 2 pounds, 2 ounces, 3. 152 ounces; 9 pounds, 8 ounces, 4. 128 ounces; 8 pounds, 5. 120 ounces; 7 pounds, 8 ounces; 6. answers will vary but must total 40 ounces.

158–159 Liquid Lunch: 1 cup + 1 cup = 2 cups = 1 pint; Sip o' Soda: 8 pints ÷ 2 = 4 pints = 1 gallon; Lemony Limeade: 2 cups = 1 pint, 1 pint + 1 pint = 2 pints = 1 quart; Best Broth: 1 pint + 1 pint = 1 quart + 1 quart = 2 quarts = $\frac{1}{2}$ gallon + $\frac{1}{2}$ gallon = 1 gallon; Slippery Salad Dressing: 2 pints = 1 quart, 1 quart + 1 quart = 1 half gallon

160–161 1. liters, 2. centimeters, 3. meters, 4. kilograms, 5. kilometers, 6. decimeters

162–163 ghoul-oshes; they get flaky; fewer; 30°C, Fahrenheit

164–165 foot, clock, length, ruler, day, hour, year, gram, scale, thermometer, tablespoon, quart, pound, millimeter, minute, inch, month, pint, centimeter, gallon, yard, decade, mile, ounce; **see below**

164–165

The Right Angle

Aren't these baby birds cute? Some are acute, too! Find out which ones. Try fitting the corner of a sheet of paper—which forms a right angle—into each baby bird's mouth.

If the paper just fits, the mouth forms a right angle. A **right angle** looks like the corner of a square.

If there's room to spare in the baby bird's mouth, the angle is obtuse. An **obtuse angle** is wider than a right angle.

And if the baby bird's mouth is hidden by the page, the angle is acute. An **acute angle** is narrower than a right angle.

Try the paper measure. Then write **acute**, **obtuse**, or **right** next to each baby bird.

_____   _____   _____

_____

_____

_____

_____

_____

Now label the angles in these pairs. Write **>**, **<**, or **=** to show how they compare in angle width.

Triangles with a Point

Color all of the right-triangle-shaped signs **red**.
Color all of the equilateral-triangle-shaped signs **yellow**.
Color all of the isosceles-triangle-shaped signs **green**.

Triangle: a shape with 3 sides and 3 corners

Isosceles Triangle: a triangle with only two sides the same length

Right triangle: a triangle in which 2 of the line segments meet to form a right angle

Equilateral Triangle: a triangle with all 3 sides the same length

SCHOOL ZONE

watch out for MONSTERS

NEXT REST STOP: 20 MILES

Cow Crossing

Chicken Crossing

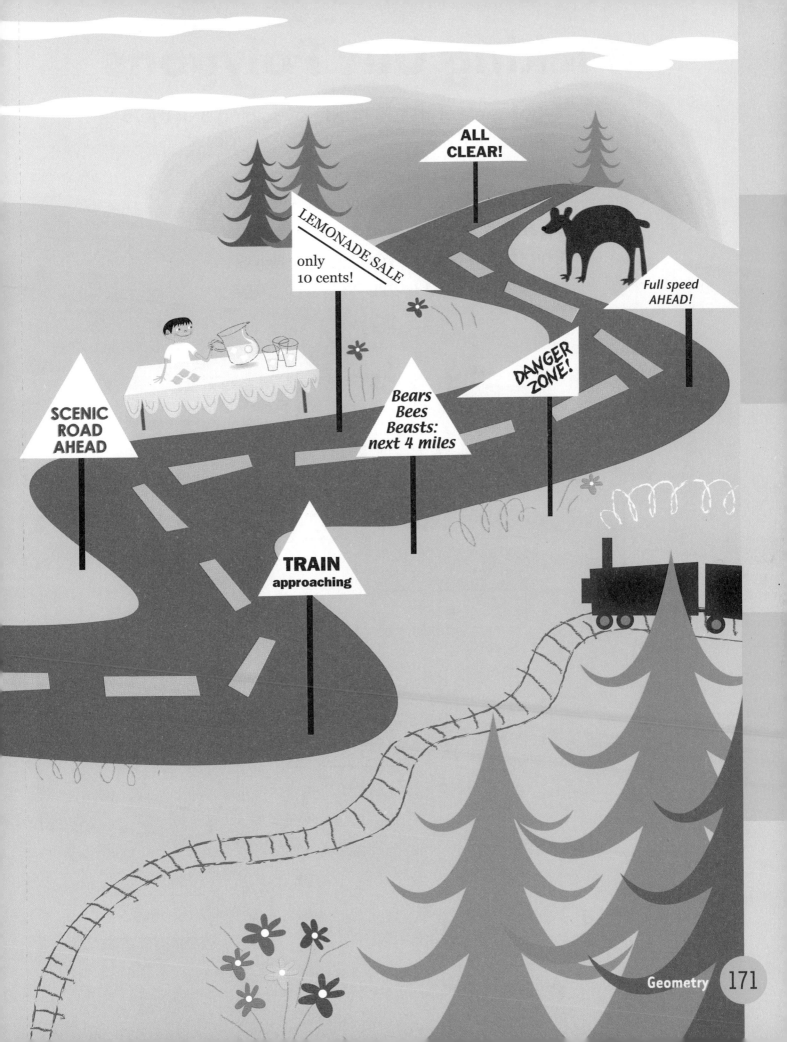

Picking Out Polygons

A **polygon** is a flat shape made by joining 3 or more line segments. These shapes are all polygons:

A **triangle** is a polygon with 3 sides.

A **quadrilateral** is a polygon with 4 sides.

A **pentagon** is a polygon with 5 sides.

A **hexagon** is a polygon with 6 sides.

An **octagon** is a polygon with 8 sides.

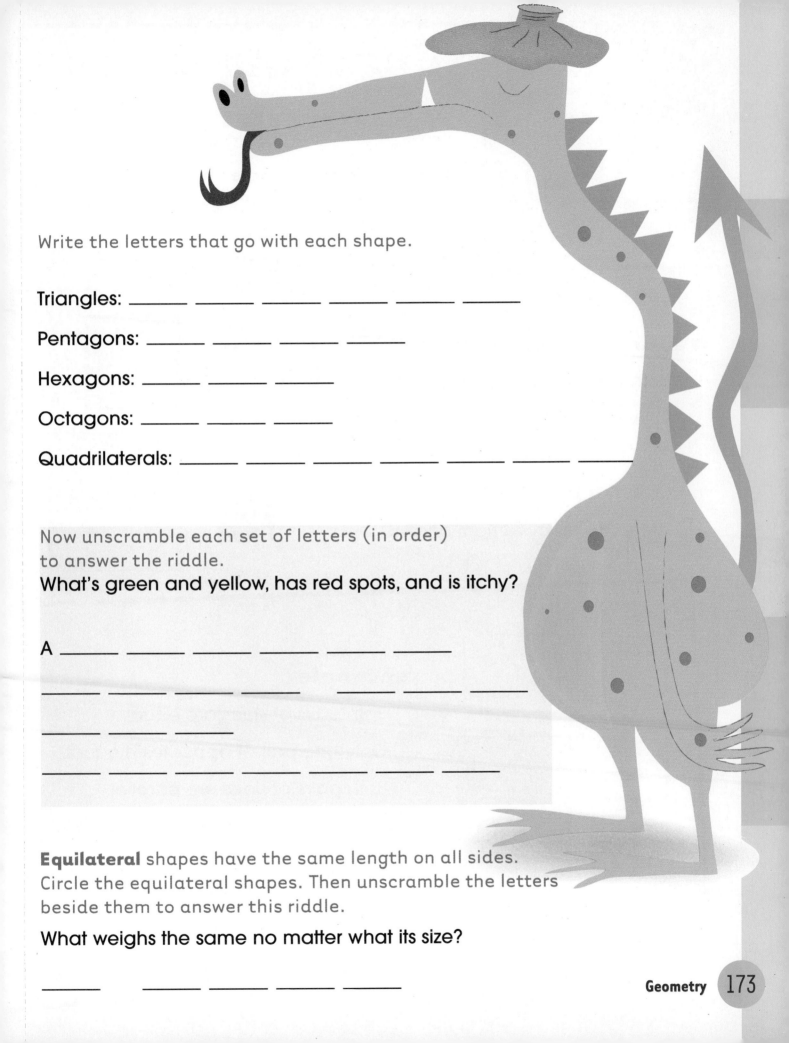

Write the letters that go with each shape.

Triangles: ____ ____ ____ ____ ____ ____

Pentagons: ____ ____ ____ ____

Hexagons: ____ ____ ____

Octagons: ____ ____ ____

Quadrilaterals: ____ ____ ____ ____ ____ ____

Now unscramble each set of letters (in order)
to answer the riddle.

What's green and yellow, has red spots, and is itchy?

A ____ ____ ____ ____ ____ ____

____ ____ ____ ____ ____ ____

____ ____ ____

____ ____ ____ ____ ____

Equilateral shapes have the same length on all sides.
Circle the equilateral shapes. Then unscramble the letters
beside them to answer this riddle.

What weighs the same no matter what its size?

____ ____ ____ ____ ____

Checking Up on Quadrilaterals

All the shapes shown here are **quadrilaterals** — polygons with 4 sides. Check the statements that are true about each group of quadrilaterals.

square

- ◯ Both pairs of sides are equal.
- ◯ Only one pair of opposites is equal.
- ◯ Both pairs of sides are parallel.
- ◯ Only one pair of opposites is parallel.
- ◯ There are always 4 right angles.

rectangle

- ◯ Both pairs of sides are equal.
- ◯ Only one pair of opposites is equal.
- ◯ Both pairs of sides are parallel.
- ◯ Only one pair of opposites is parallel.
- ◯ There are always 4 right angles.

rhombus

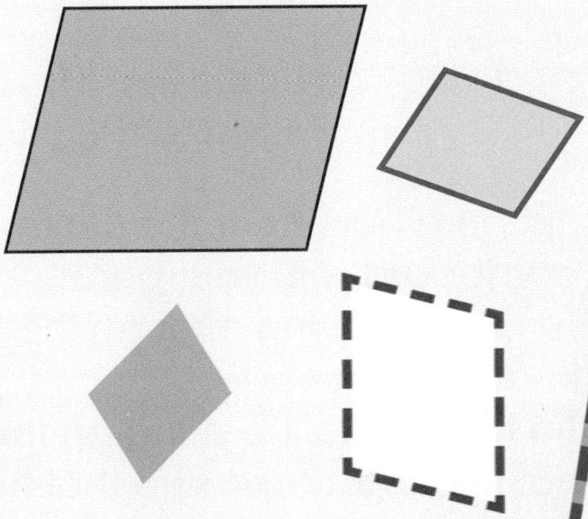

- ◯ Both pairs of sides are equal.
- ◯ Only one pair of opposites is equal.
- ◯ Both pairs of sides are parallel.
- ◯ Only one pair of opposites is parallel.
- ◯ There are always 4 right angles.

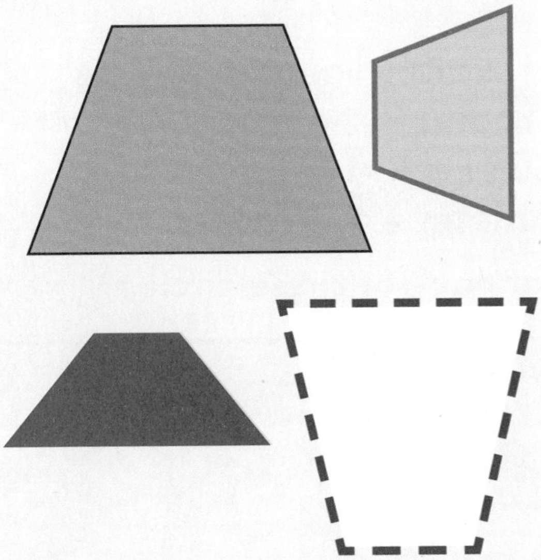

trapezoid

- ◯ Both pairs of sides are equal.
- ◯ Only one pair of opposites is equal.
- ◯ Both pairs of sides are parallel.
- ◯ Only one pair of opposites is parallel.
- ◯ There are always 4 right angles.

In a **parallelogram**, both pair of sides are parallel. Which sets of shapes shown here are also parallelograms? _____

_____

Going Around in Circles

A **circle** is a flat, perfectly round shape. Draw your own perfect circle using a pen, string, and a piece of cardboard. Here's how.

1. Punch a hole near the center of the cardboard with your pen.
2. Thread the string through the hole, and knot it on one side.
3. Tie the pen to the string on the side that is not knotted. Make sure that the pen will not reach beyond the edge of the cardboard. Then stretch the pen out, and draw! The knot in the string will keep the pen an equal distance from the center point as you draw.

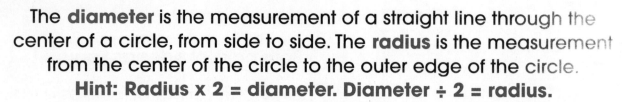

The **diameter** is the measurement of a straight line through the center of a circle, from side to side. The **radius** is the measurement from the center of the circle to the outer edge of the circle.
Hint: Radius x 2 = diameter. Diameter ÷ 2 = radius.

What is the radius and the diameter of each of these circles?

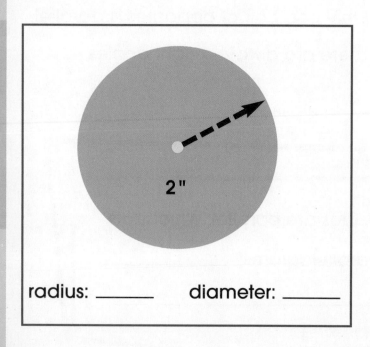

2"

radius: _____   diameter: _____

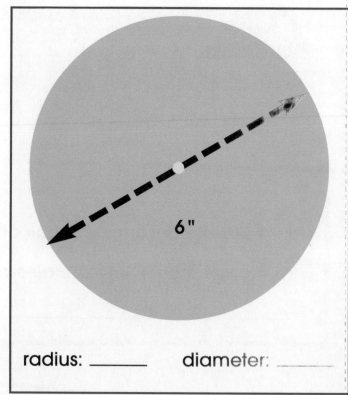

6"

radius: _____   diameter: _____

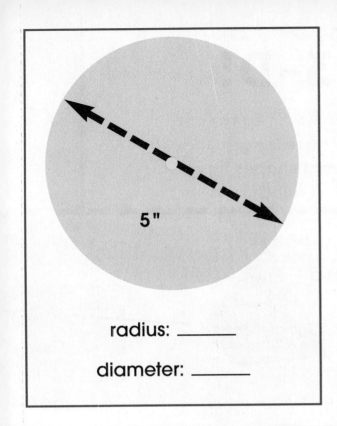

5"

radius: _____

diameter: _____

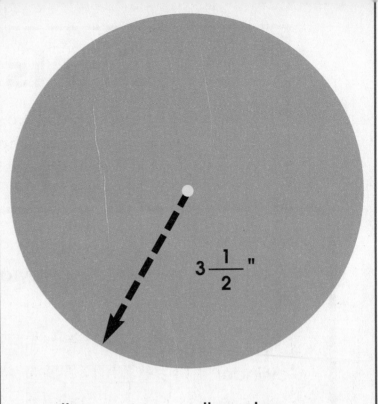

$3\frac{1}{2}$ "

radius: _____   diameter: _____

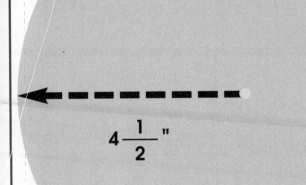

$4\frac{1}{2}$ "

radius: _____   diameter: _____

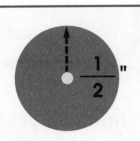

$\frac{1}{2}$ "

radius: _____

diameter: _____

Life Is 3-D!

The shapes you've worked with so far are **two-dimensional**: they have length and width. **Three-dimensional** shapes have length, width, *and* depth.

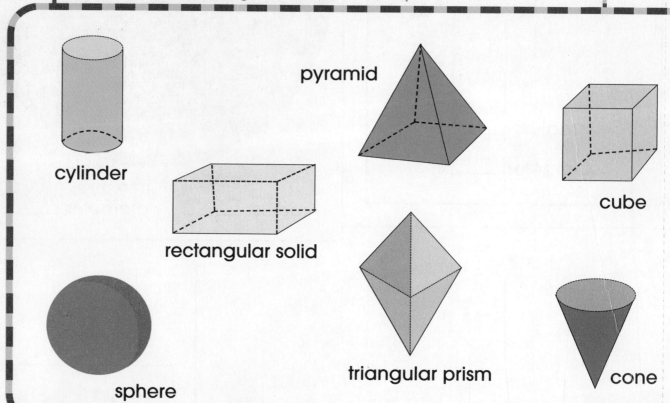

cylinder

pyramid

cube

rectangular solid

sphere

triangular prism

cone

How many sides does a rectangular solid have? _____

What is the bottom of the pyramid shaped like? _____

Which of these shapes is likely to roll? _____

How many sides does a cube have? _____

Which of these shapes could support another of the same

shape on top of it? _____

Write the name of the shape or shapes that describes each of these objects.

_____

_____

_____

_____

_____

_____

A Totally Cubular Puzzle

A **cube** has six square sides. Which of these diagrams could be folded into a cube? Circle the letter next to the ones you think will work. Then use cardboard, tape, and a pair of scissors to see if you were right!

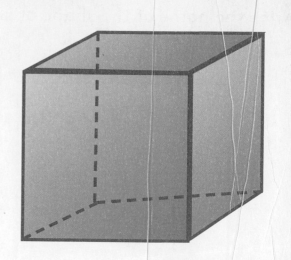

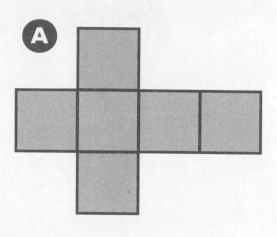

A

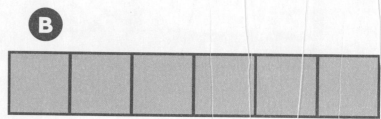

B

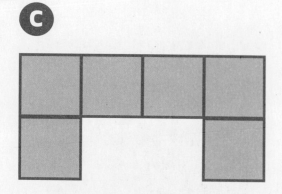

C

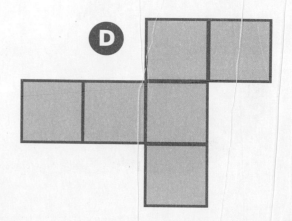

D

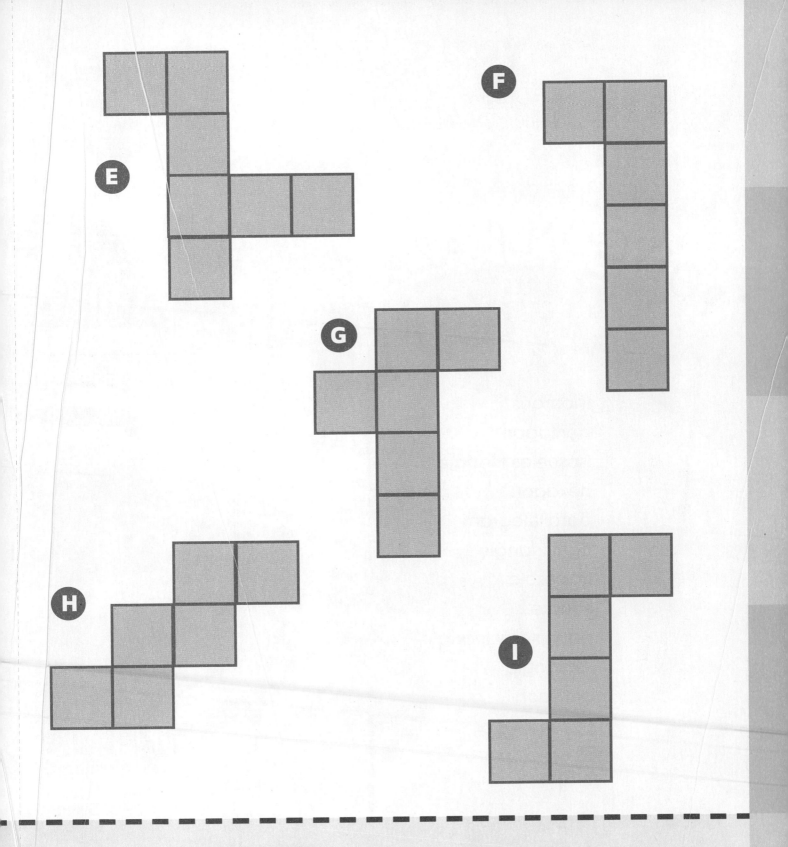

Bonus: What do all the diagrams that fold into a cube have in common?

_____

Polygon Plaza

Write a shape word next to the building it describes.
Choose from the words in the polygon plaza.

POLYGON PLAZA

rhombus
pentagon
isosceles triangle
hexagon
parallelogram
right triangle
trapezoid
square
equilateral triangle
rectangle
octagon

THREE SIDES STREET

EIGHT SIDES BLVD.

SIX SIDES AVENUE

PARALLEL PATH

FOUR SIDES ROAD

PARTIALLY PARALLEL PATH

FIVE SIDES HIGHWAY

The Same . . . Only Different

Tina sat at the kitchen table doodling. Her mom had told her to sit there quietly until she learned to play nicely with her little brother, Jamal. "This isn't fair!" Tina thought. "Why does Jamal always have to tag along, acting like a copycat?"

"Can I draw with you?" There he was *again!* Jamal pulled up a chair without waiting for an answer.

Tina moved her chair away from her brother. She wordlessly tore a sheet of paper from her drawing pad and handed it to him. Jamal immediately started copying Tina's doodles. Tina sighed. Then she couldn't help herself. She peeked over at what Jamal was doing. Some of his shapes really did look exactly like hers. But others—well, they needed work.

"Tell you what, Jamal," Tina said. "Some of your shapes look **congruent** with mine. That means they are the exact same size and shape. If we cut them out and placed yours on top of mine, they would match exactly. Some of your other shapes, though, are not congruent with mine. They don't even look similar. If you can change those shapes into ones that are similar—that have the same shape as mine, even if the size is different—I'll take you to the park."

"Really? You promise?" Jamal asked.

"I promise," Tina answered. "But remember: All your shapes have to be either congruent or similar to mine. And you can't draw new ones. You have to work with what you've already drawn. If you can do it, I'll take you to the park. If not, you have to leave me alone the rest of the day. Is it a deal?"

Jamal looked at his older sister. Was she trying to trick him? He studied Tina's sheet of drawings and then his own.

"Okay," Jamal agreed. "It's a deal."

Did Jamal get to go to the park? Figure out the answer:
Put an **X** through all the **congruent** shapes.

Are the remaining shapes similar? _____

Remember:

Congruent shapes are exactly the same as one another in both size and shape.

Similar shapes have the same shape but are not necessarily the same size.

Tina

Jamal

Congruent shapes are always similar—but similar shapes are not always congruent. Can you explain why that is?

_____

Number Lines

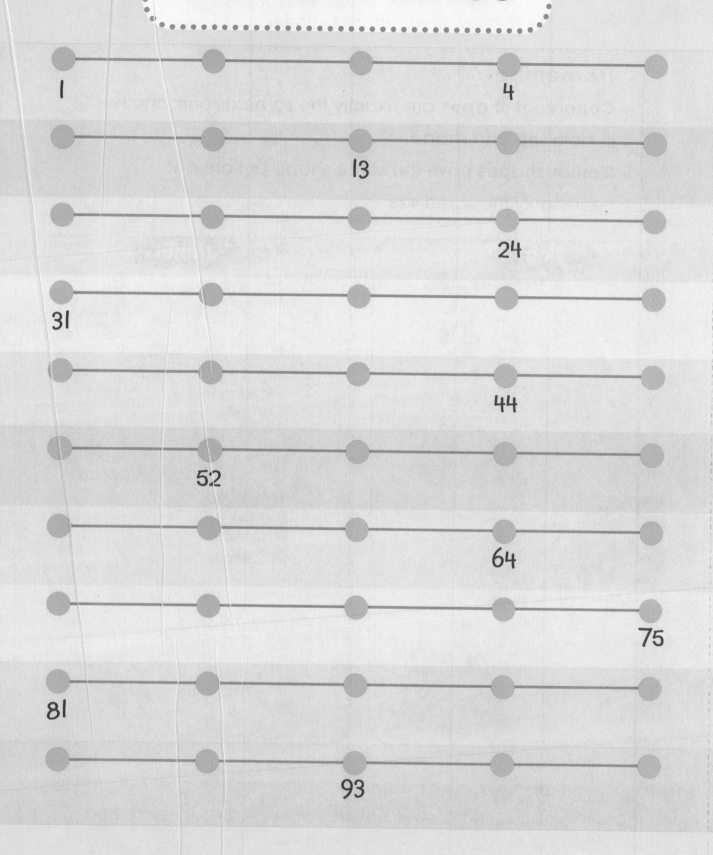

1   4

13

24

31

44

52

64

75

81

93

Write the missing numbers on the number line under each point.

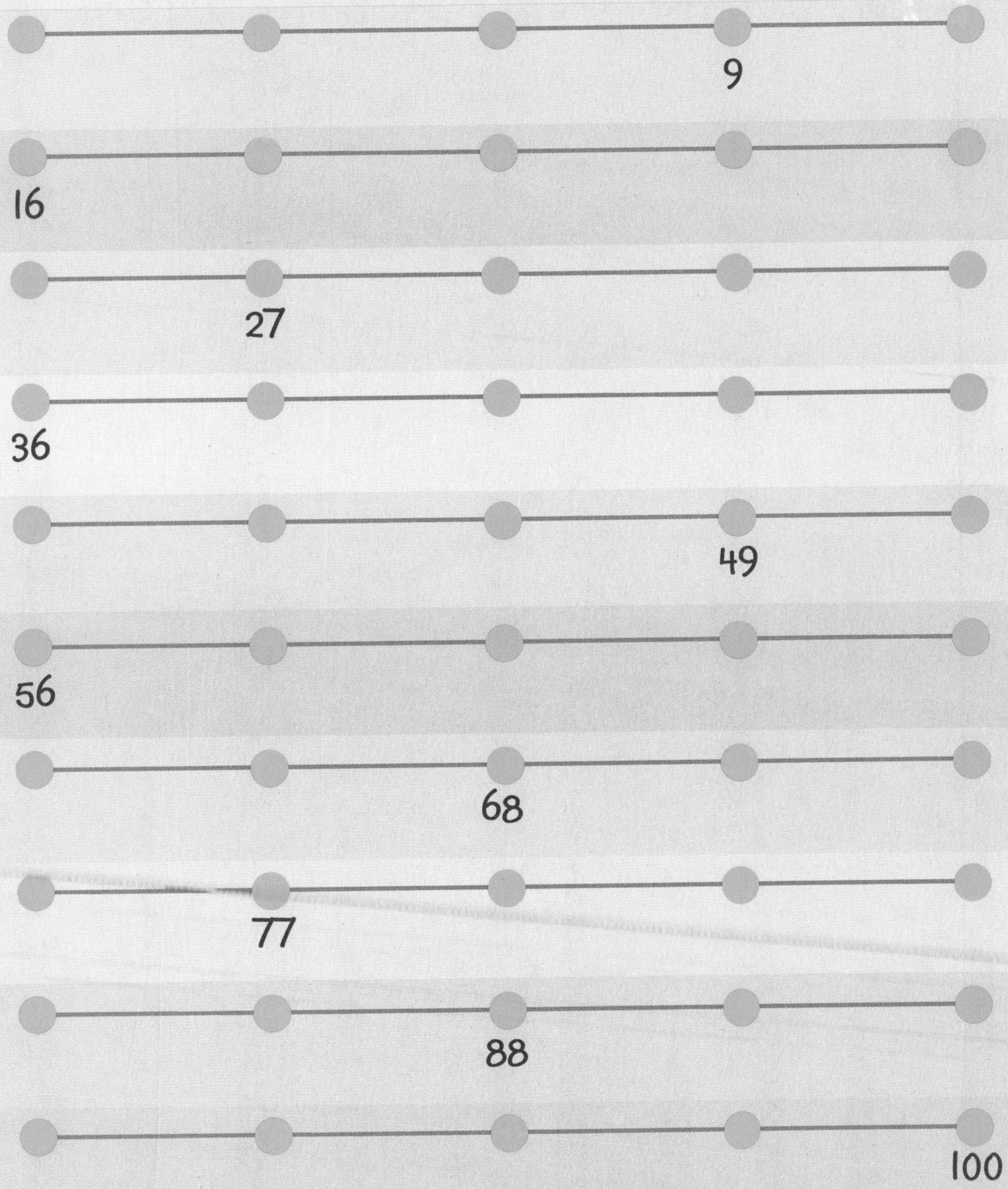
9
16
27
36
49
56
68
77
88
100

Circle your age on the number line. Circle the age of an older relative.

How many points between your ages? ____

Snake in the Grass

Fill in the numbers on the number line counting up by $\frac{1}{2}$s.
Then use the letters that mark some of the points to answer the riddle.

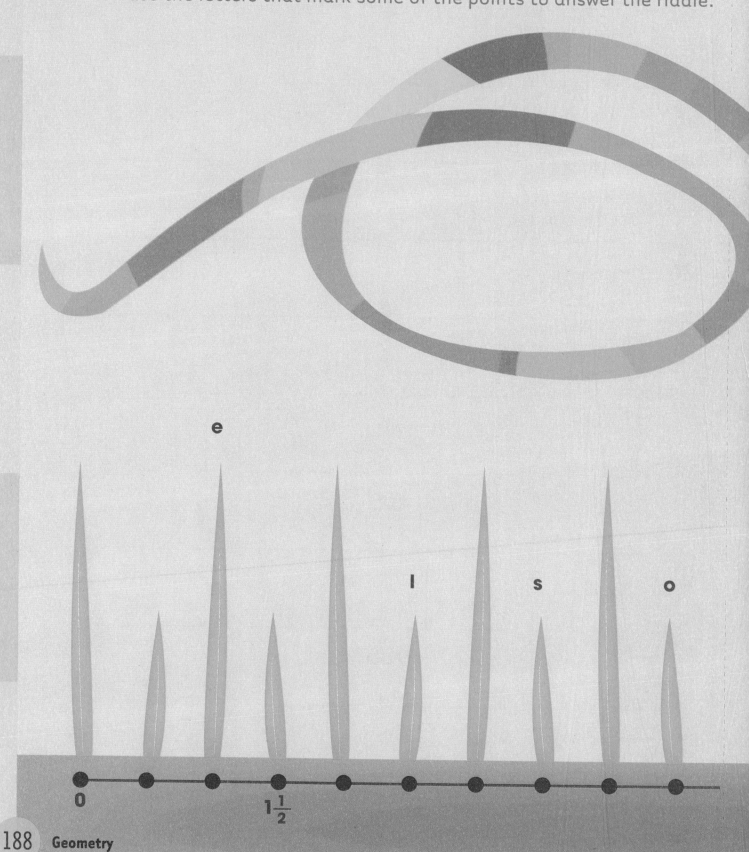

0

$1\frac{1}{2}$

What does a snake write at the end of its letters?

$$\overline{} \; \overline{} \; \overline{} \; \overline{}$$
$$2\frac{1}{2} \quad 4\frac{1}{2} \quad 6 \quad 1$$

$$\overline{} \; \overline{} \; \overline{}$$
$$9 \quad 10 \quad 7\frac{1}{2}$$

$$\overline{} \; \overline{} \; \overline{} \; \overline{} \; \overline{} \; \overline{}$$
$$5\frac{1}{2} \quad 8\frac{1}{2} \quad 3\frac{1}{2} \quad 3\frac{1}{2} \quad 1 \quad 3\frac{1}{2}$$

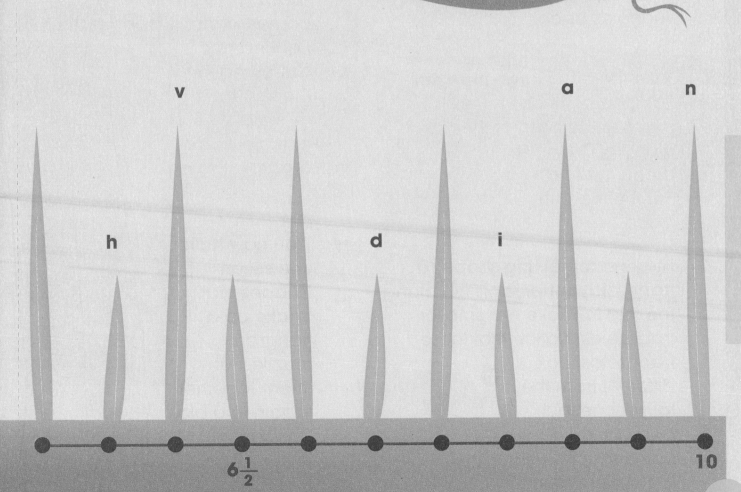

v · a · n · h · d · i

$6\frac{1}{2}$ · 10

Tangrams

A **tangram** is a geometric puzzle with seven pieces. You can use the pieces to make pictures. Here's how to make a tangram.

You Need • a square sheet of paper (or a square cut out of a piece of paper) • a pair of scissors

1. Fold a square sheet of paper in half along the diagonal. Cut along the fold. Now you have two right triangles.

2. Fold one of the two triangles in half. Cut along the fold, and put these two triangles aside.

3. Take the other large triangle. Fold the point down until it touches the base of the triangle. Cut along the fold. Put the triangle aside.

2. cut
1. fold

4. Fold the remaining shape (a trapezoid) in half, and cut along the fold to make two smaller trapezoids. Notice that these trapezoids look different from the larger one, but they are still 4-sided shapes with 2 parallel sides.

5. Lay down one trapezoid as shown. Fold its bottom left corner so that it touches the bottom right corner. Cut along the fold to make a triangle and a square. Put these two shapes aside.

2. cut
1. fold

6. Hold the other trapezoid as shown. Fold the bottom left corner so that it touches the top right corner. Cut along the fold to make a triangle and a parallelogram.

1. fold
2. cut

7. You now have the seven shapes that make up a tangram puzzle. Put them together again in a big square.

What figures can you make? Hint: Try a cat, a swan, or a goose.

Geometry Answer Key

Note: Answers read across, per page.

168–169 right; obtuse; obtuse; acute; right; acute; obtuse; obtuse; right < obtuse; acute < right; acute = acute; right > acute; right < obtuse

170–171 **red:** Danger Zone!, Train Approaching, Chicken Crossing, Lemonade Sale: Only 10 cents!; **yellow:** Cow Crossing, School Zone, Bears, Bees, Beasts Next 4 Miles, Scenic Road Ahead; **green:** All Clear! Full Speed Ahead!, Watch Out for Monsters, Run for the Hills!, Next Rest Stop 20 Miles

172–173 Letter order may vary: **triangles:** d, a, o, r, g, n; **pentagons:** a, h, t, t; **hexagons:** a, h, s; **octagons:** e, h, t; **quadrilaterals:** a, e, m, s, e, l, s; dragon that has the measles; a hole

174–175 **square:** check 1st, 3rd, and 5th boxes; **rectangle:** check 2nd, 3rd, and 5th boxes; **rhombus:** check 1st and 3rd boxes; **trapezoid,:** check 2nd and 4th boxes; squares, rectangles, rhombuses

176–177 2, 4; 3, 6; $2\frac{1}{2}$, 5; $3\frac{1}{2}$, 7; $4\frac{1}{2}$, 9; $\frac{1}{2}$, 1

178–179 6, a square, a cylinder and a sphere, 6, a cylinder, a rectangular solid, and a cube; triangular prism, cube, rectangular solid, sphere and cone, sphere, pyramid

180–181 Circle: A, D, E, G, H, I; all must have 6 squares with 2 that stick out on opposite sides.

182–183 **See below.**

184–185 Put an X on yellow rectangles; green rhombuses; red pentagrams; orange triangles; yes; similar shapes can have same shape, but not size.

186–187 Write in the numbers as directed.

188–189 Write in the numbers; love and hisses

182–183

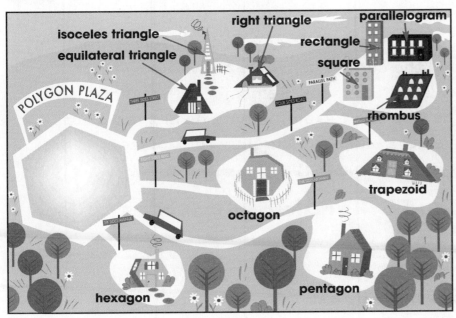

Watch Out!

There's a blueberry thief at Camp Goodfood! At exactly 11:30 A.M., Chef Sherlock arrived at the camp kitchen to prepare lunch. He was going to make blueberry pie for dessert.

When the chef walked through the front door of the kitchen, he saw someone run out the back door. Chef Sherlock looked around the kitchen. His big bowl of blueberries was missing! The chef went sniffing around outside. Footsteps and a trail of blueberry stains all pointed to Bunk 5. Chef Sherlock was certain that one of the campers in that bunk was the blueberry burglar.

Read what Bunk 5's campers have to say for themselves. Then use these clues and the camp's schedule of events to track down Chef Sherlock's lead suspect. Remember: The culprit is likely to be someone who can't explain where he or she was at 11:30 A.M., when the blueberry burglary took place!

Camp Goodfood Schedule of Activities

Swimming: 9:00 A.M.–10:30 A.M.

Quiet Time: 10:30 A.M.–11:00 A.M.

Horseback Riding: 11:00 A.M.–1:00 P.M.

Lunch: 1:00 P.M.–2:00 P.M.

All-Day Options: hiking, Ping-Pong, arts and crafts

Camper 1: "For the last hour, I've been playing Ping-Pong."

Camper 2: "After horseback riding, I went to lunch."

Camper 3: "In arts and crafts, I made this toy watch showing the time I finished it."

Camper 4: "I fell asleep during quiet time and didn't wake up until the lunch bell rang."

Camper 5: "I left to go hiking about a half hour after I woke up, which was 9 A.M. It took me an hour to hike up the mountain and only a half hour to climb back down."

Camper 6: "Who, me? I slept late. By the time I woke up, most of the kids were just getting back from horseback riding. So I just waited for them in the bunk. Then I went to lunch."

Who would you say is the lead suspect? _____

Why do you think that is? _____

_____

Fractions of a Dollar

What do a $1.00 bill and fractions have in common? Find out! Using a different color crayon or marker for each type of coin, color in the fraction of the bill on this page that each coin below is worth. The information at the right will help you.

 1 penny (1¢) = $\frac{1}{100}$ of $1.00

 1 nickel (5¢) = $\frac{5}{100}$ (or $\frac{1}{20}$) of $1.00

 1 dime (10¢) = $\frac{10}{100}$ (or $\frac{1}{10}$) of $1.00

 1 quarter (25¢) = $\frac{25}{100}$ (or $\frac{1}{4}$) of $1.00

Answer these questions about the coins on page 194.

What is the total value of the coins? _____

How does the fraction of the $1.00 bill that you've colored in

and the amount of money shown compare? _____

_____

Another way of writing one cent is $.01.
Another way of writing one dollar and one cent is $1.01.

Use decimals numbers to write the following amounts.

five dollars and sixty-two cents _____

eight dollars and ninety-nine cents _____

seven dollars and fifty cents _____

three dollars and twenty-three cents _____

three dollars and thirty-two cents _____

ten dollars and two cents _____

The Perfect-Pet Price Club

Answer the questions using the prices in the window.
Look in the box if you need help.

> To add money amounts that end in .99, round up to the next whole dollar. Then subtract that number of pennies from your final total.
>
> **Example:** $8.99 + $6.99
>
> Think: $9.00 + $7.00 = $16.00 − 2¢ (1¢ from each item) = $15.98

What is the cost of 2 claw clippers? _____

If you used a $10.00 bill to buy a bag of Yummy Bites, how much

change would you get back? _____

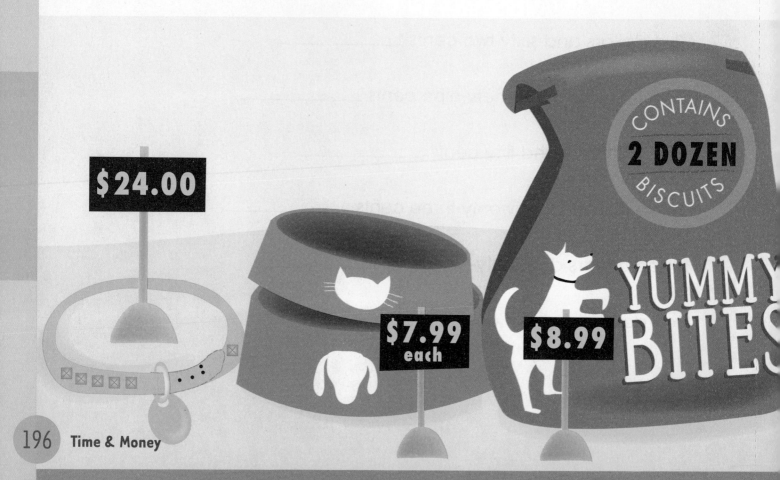

$24.00

$7.99
each

$8.99

YUMMY BITES

CONTAINS 2 DOZEN BISCUITS

Fido and Fifi really need new dog dishes and collars. How much will it cost to get them these items? _____

How much would 2 boxes of Way-Too-Good Treats cost at the regular price? _____

How much would you save by buying 2 boxes of Way Too Good Treats at the sale price? _____

The Perfect-Pet Price Club is holding a sale!
All items are half off!

How much would it cost you to buy a rhinestone dog collar and a doghouse during this half-price sale?

_____

ON SALE
2 boxes
for $4.50

regularly
$2.29 each

WAY TOO
GOOD
TREATS

$3.99

$75.00

What a Year!

Write the answers to these questions on the lines below.

1. What month comes right before December?

_____ _____ _____ ◯ _____ _____ _____

2. What do you call a year containing 366 days?

_____ _____ ◯ _____ _____ _____

3. How many months of the year end in the letter **r**?

___ ___ ___ ( )

4. In what month is Halloween celebrated?

___ ( ) ___ ___ ___ ___ ___

5. What is the third month of the year? ___ ___ ___ ___ ( )

6. What day of the week comes after Thursday?

( ) ___ ___ ___ ___ ___

7. How many days are there in the last two months of the year, combined?

___ ___ ___ ___ ___-( ) ___ ___

8. What month of the year sometimes has 28 days in it and sometimes has 29? ___ ___ ___ ( ) ___ ___ ___ ___

9. How many years are there in a decade? ( ) ___ ___

10. How many years are there in a century?

___ ___ ___ ( ) ___ ___ ___ ___ ___

Now write the circled lettters in order to answer the riddle below

When does Parade Day take place?

___ ___ ___ ___ ___

___ ___ ___ ___ ___

Be a Quick-Change Artist!

See how quickly you can answer these questions. Then ask a friend the same questions, and see which of you is the quickest quick-change artist around!

What's the best way to give someone change of $1.00 using exactly

2 coins? _____

3 coins? _____

4 coins? _____

5 coins? _____

6 coins? _____

8 coins? _____

13 coins? _____

Increase the number of coins and the dollar amount you're making change of, and play again.

Time & Money Answer Key

192–193 Camper 5; she got back from hiking at 11:00 A.M. and does not explain where she was after that.

194–195 **pennies:** 5 squares colored in, **nickels:** 5 squares colored in, **dimes:** 40 squares colored in, **quarters:** 50 squares colored in; $1.00, 100 squares are colored in, 100 squares = $1.00; $5.62, $8.99, $7,50, $3.23, $3.32, $10.02

196–197 $7.98, $1.01, $63.98, $4.58, 8¢, $47.00

198–199 1. November, 2. leap year, 3. four, 4. October, 5. March, 6. Friday, 7. sixty-one, 8. February, 9. ten, 10. one hundred; march forth

3, 2, 1 . . . Lift Off!

Counting backward by ones is a common pattern in space flight. But what pattern is on each of these rockets? Write the next three numbers in each pattern. Then, in the space beneath each rocket, describe the pattern in your own words.

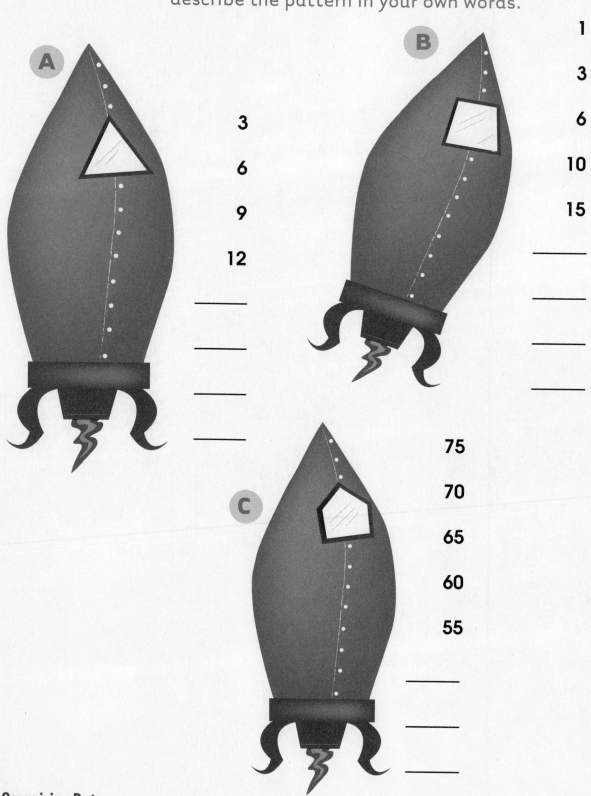

A

3
6
9
12
___
___
___
___

B

1
3
6
10
15
___
___
___

C

75
70
65
60
55
___
___
___

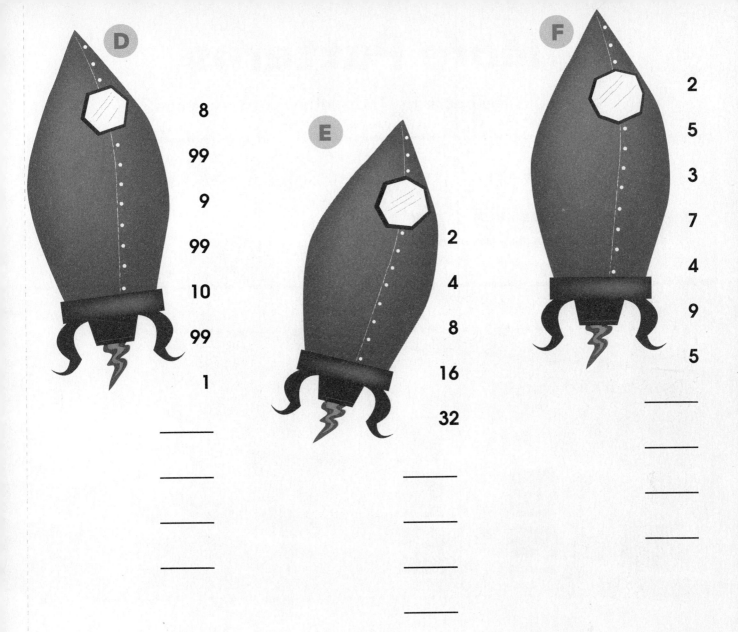

D

8
99
9
99
10
99
1

____

____

____

____

E

2
4
8
16
32

____

____

____

____

F

2
5
3
7
4
9
5

____

____

____

Shapes and designs can follow patterns, just as numbers can. What pattern do the rocket windows on these rocket ships follow? What should the next rocket window shape look like?

_____

More Patterns

Look at the patterns. Then follow the directions.

Draw the next 3 things.

Draw the next thing.

Draw the next 3 things.

Draw the next 4 cars in the last row.

Draw the next group.

Write the next three numbers.

2   6   12   20   30   _____   _____   _____

Write the next three fractions.

$\frac{1}{2}$ $\frac{2}{4}$ $\frac{3}{6}$ $\frac{4}{8}$ $\frac{5}{10}$ _____   _____   _____

Write the next three numbers.

1   4   9   16   25   _____   _____   _____

Pete has been trying to improve his swimming time. It took him 2 minutes to swim a lap on Monday. It took him 1 minute and 58 seconds on Tuesday. It took him 1 minute and 56 seconds on Wednesday. If he continues to improve his time by 2 seconds every day, how long will it take him to swim a lap on Sunday?

_____

Dot's a Square?

The numbers 1, 3, and 6 are called **triangular numbers** because you can arrange these numbers of dots or items into a triangle shape, like this:

1	3	6
(1)	(1 + 2)	(1 + 2 + 3)

  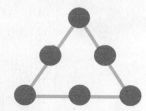

What should the next triangular number be? _____ Draw it!

The numbers 1, 4, and 9 are called **square numbers**. Notice how each of these number of dots can form a square:

1	4	9
(1 x 1)	(2 x 2)	(3 x 3)

What should the next square number be? _____ Draw it!

Draw dots to find other triangular and square numbers.
Use what you learn to complete this chart. Write **yes** or **no**
in the correct column next to each number.

Number	Triangular	Square
3		
4		
6		
9		
10		
15		
16		
21		
25		
28		
36		

Which number is both triangular and square? _____

Likely / Unlikely?

Likely events will probably happen. For example, the sun is likely to rise tomorrow.

Unlikely events will probably not happen. For example, it is unlikely that the president of the United States will ring your doorbell this afternoon.

Impossible events cannot happen. For example, it is impossible for the furniture to talk.

Circle the letter next to the events that are **likely**. Put a slash through the letter next to the events that are **unlikely**. Put an **X** through the letter next to the events that are **impossible**.

m. You'll fly in a rocket to the moon before your 25th birthday.

e. A dog will bark today somewhere in your neighborhood.

o. You will grow 6 inches by tomorrow morning.

p. All the computers in the world will stop working tomorrow.

o. If you start counting stars in the sky when they come out tonight, you will be done by your bedtime.

t. Cows will start giving strawberry-flavored milk.

o. If you put water in a working freezer, it will turn to ice.

o. If you pet a kitten it will start purring.

e. If you roll one regular 6-sided die, it will land on the number 7.

a. The sun will rise in the west tomorrow morning, and set in the east.

c. You will receive a phone call saying that you have just won $1,000.

l. You will throw a ball up in the air—and it will never come down.

c. Flowers will grow behind your ears.

c. Some magic words you say will cause your best friend to disappear.

h. You will see someone doing cartwheels across your street today.

c. It will rain at some point within the next month.

i. It will snow in most areas of the United States on July 4.

k. If the clock in your room says 3:00, in an hour it will say 4:00.

i. After you go to sleep, you will wake up at some point within the next 24 hours.

h. If you put a rock in a bowl of water, it will float.

s. If you eat too much candy, you'll get a stomachache.

Unscramble each set of letters to answer this riddle.

What is a monkey's favorite dessert?

Unscramble the **impossible** events.

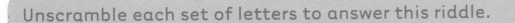
____ ____ ____ ____ ____ ____ ____ ____

Unscramble the **unlikely** events.

____ ____ ____ ____ ____

Unscramble the **likely** events.

____ ____ ____ ____ ____ ____

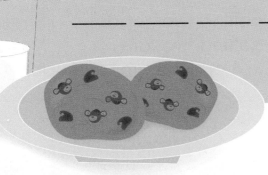

Flip a Coin

When you flip a coin, it comes up heads or tails. There's 1 chance in 2 of either side appearing. This means that if you flip a coin over and over again, it will, in the long run, come up heads and tails about the same number of times.

Try it! Flip a coin 50 times.
Use this grid to keep track of what happens.

H for heads
T for tails

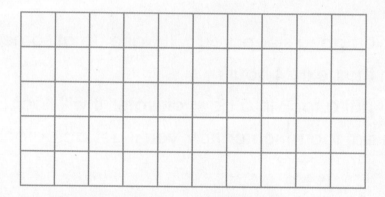

How many times did the coin come up heads?_____

How many times did the coin come up tails? _____

What happens if you flip two coins, one at a time? In this case there are 4 possible outcomes:
  You could get heads on both coins.
  You could get tails on both coins.
  You could get heads on the first coin and tails on the second.
  You could get tails on the first coin and heads on the second.

That means
  • there is 1 chance in 4 of getting two heads
  • there is 1 chance in 4 of getting two tails
  • but there are 2 chances in 4 of getting one of each

Try it! Flip two coins 25 times or more. Put an **X** in the column of this chart that describes what happens on each coin flip.

Both Heads

Both Tails

One Head and One Tail

Does one column have more **X**'s than the others? If so, which one?

_____

Why do you think that is? _____

_____

Take Your Chances

If you roll two dice, or number cubes, is there a greater chance of rolling one number more often than the others? To find out, complete this chart. It shows all of the possible sums you can roll with dice, or number cubes. It already shows some of the number combinations that can give you each sum. See how many more combinations for each sum you can come up with.

2	3	4	5	6	7	8	9	10	11	12
1 + 1	1 + 2 2 + 1		4 + 1 1 + 4	1 + 5 5 + 1		6 + 2 2 + 6			5 + 6	

From the chart you made, which number does it seem is likely to come up more often than any other when you roll the dice?

_____

Now make another chart with the numbers 2 to 12 at the bottom. Roll a pair of dice 50 times, and write an **X** in the column that names the sum of each roll you get.

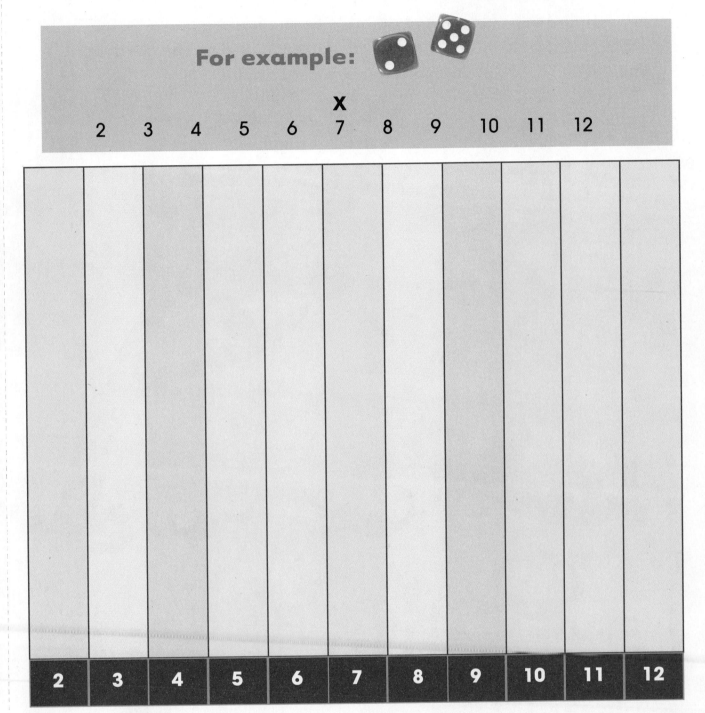

For example:

				X					
2	3	4	5	6	7	8	9	10	11	12

2	3	4	5	6	7	8	9	10	11	12

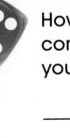

How does the shape of the data you arrived at compare with the shape of the data on your "equations chart"?

_____

Counting Critters

Help keep tabs on the animals at the nature preserve by counting the critters. Draw a bar for each one on the bar graph. Then answer the questions.

Number of Animals Counted

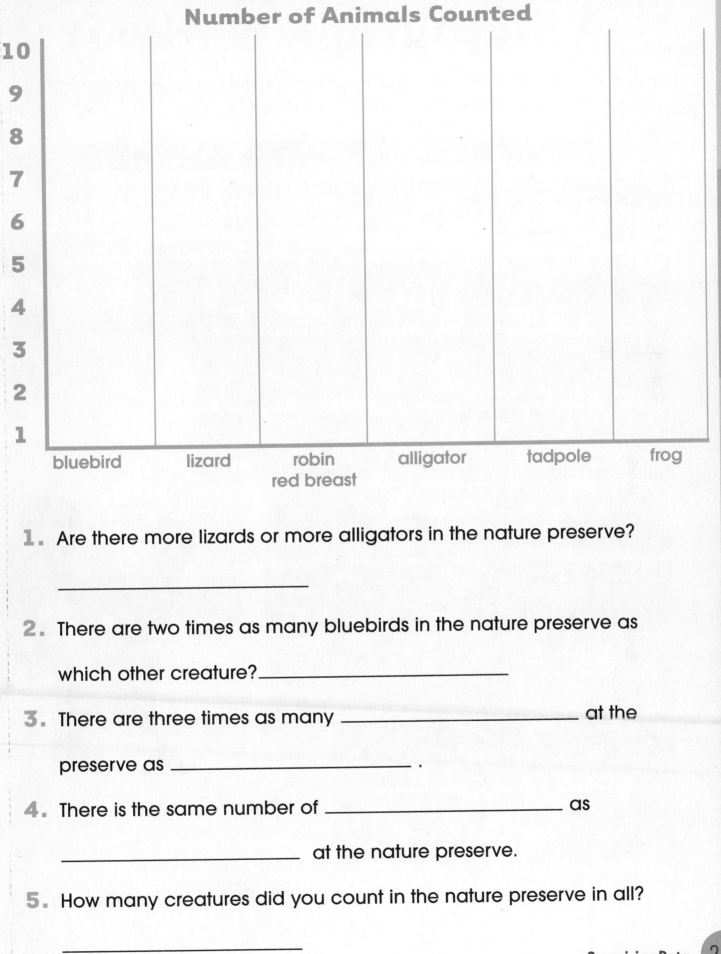

10
9
8
7
6
5
4
3
2
1

bluebird   lizard   robin
                      red breast   alligator   tadpole   frog

1. Are there more lizards or more alligators in the nature preserve?

   _____

2. There are two times as many bluebirds in the nature preserve as

   which other creature?_____

3. There are three times as many _____ at the

   preserve as _____ .

4. There is the same number of _____ as

   _____ at the nature preserve.

5. How many creatures did you count in the nature preserve in all?

   _____

A Pictograph Workout

What's your favorite ways to get exercise? Compare your answers with the ones from this recent survey.

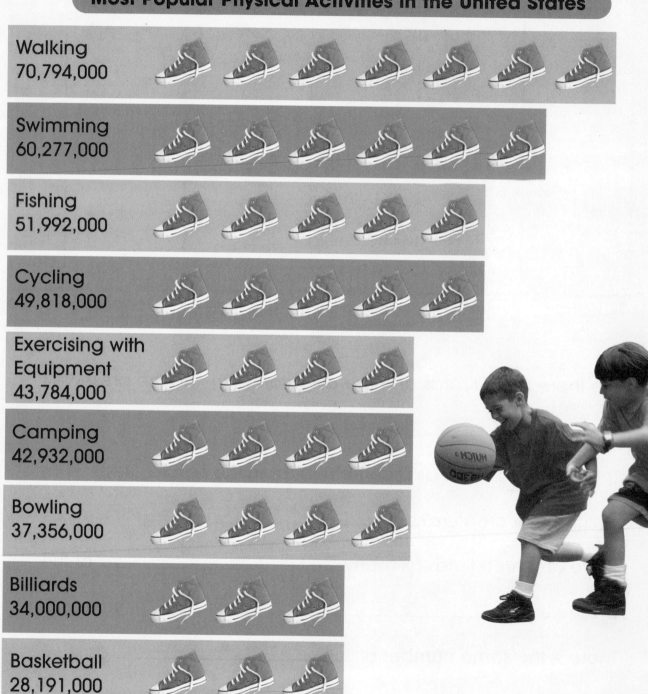

Most Popular Physical Activities in the United States

Walking
70,794,000

Swimming
60,277,000

Fishing
51,992,000

Cycling
49,818,000

Exercising with Equipment
43,784,000

Camping
42,932,000

Bowling
37,356,000

Billiards
34,000,000

Basketball
28,191,000

Source: National Sporting Goods Association.

 = 10,000,000 people

1. Each sneaker on the graph stands for

_____.

2. According to this survey, which is more popular: cycling or exercising with equipment?

_____

3. About how many people said that they like swimming?

_____

4. About how many more people said that they prefer swimming to fishing?

_____

5. After basketball, the next most popular answer given in the survey was boating. About 25,000,000 people gave this answer. Draw the number of sneakers you would need to stand for this number of people.

6. Suppose you owned a sporting-goods store. In what ways might the information on this graph be helpful to you? What else might you want to know?

_____

Mail Call!

A **line graph** makes changes over time easier to see. For example, this line graph shows increases in the price of mailing a letter. Use it to answer the questions.

Cost of Mailing a 1-ounce First-Class Letter

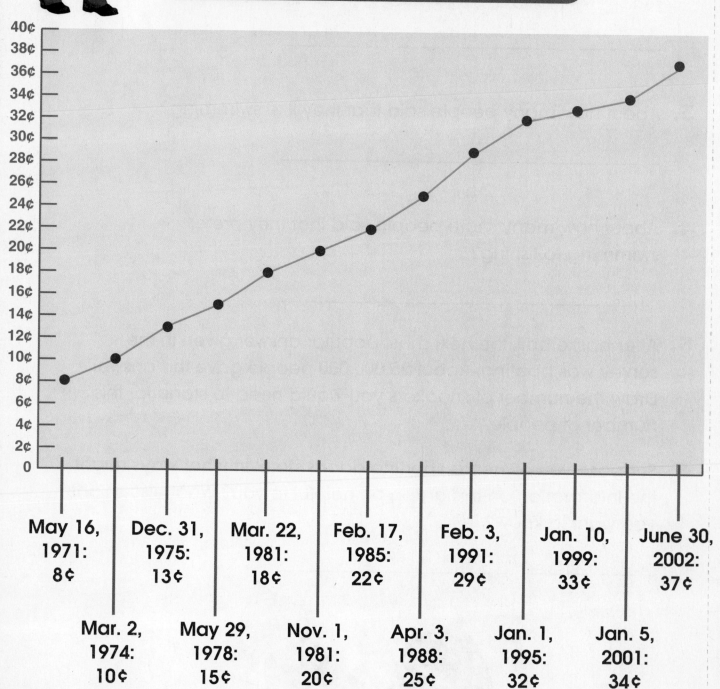

May 16, 1971: 8¢

Mar. 2, 1974: 10¢

Dec. 31, 1975: 13¢

May 29, 1978: 15¢

Mar. 22, 1981: 18¢

Nov. 1, 1981: 20¢

Feb. 17, 1985: 22¢

Apr. 3, 1988: 25¢

Feb. 3, 1991: 29¢

Jan. 1, 1995: 32¢

Jan. 10, 1999: 33¢

Jan. 5, 2001: 34¢

June 30, 2002: 37¢

1. What was the cost of mailing a 1-ounce letter as of May 29, 1978? _____

2. What was the cost of mailing a 1-ounce letter as of February 17, 1985? _____

3. How much did the price of mailing a 1-ounce letter go up between May 29, 1978, and February 17, 1985?

   _____

4. In what year did the price of mailing a 1-ounce letter go up more than once? _____

5. In what year did the largest price increase shown on the graph take place? _____

6. In April 1988, it cost 20¢ for each additional ounce that a package weighed, up to 11 ounces.

   a. How much did it cost to mail a 2-ounce letter?

      _____

   b. How much did it cost to mail a 10-ounce package?

      _____

Fair or Unfair?

Use these wacky TV dinner spinners to answer the questions.

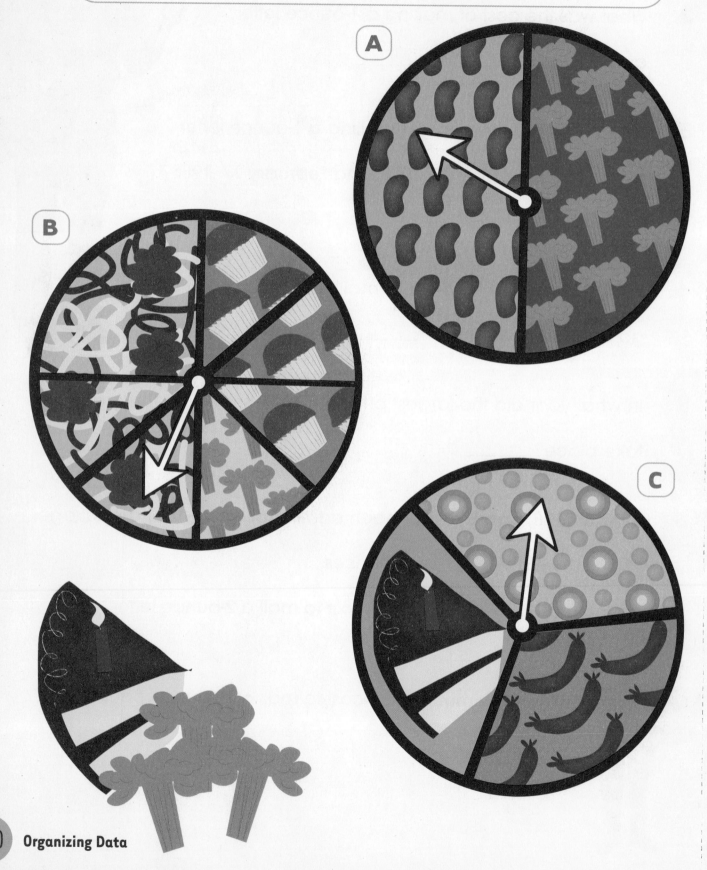

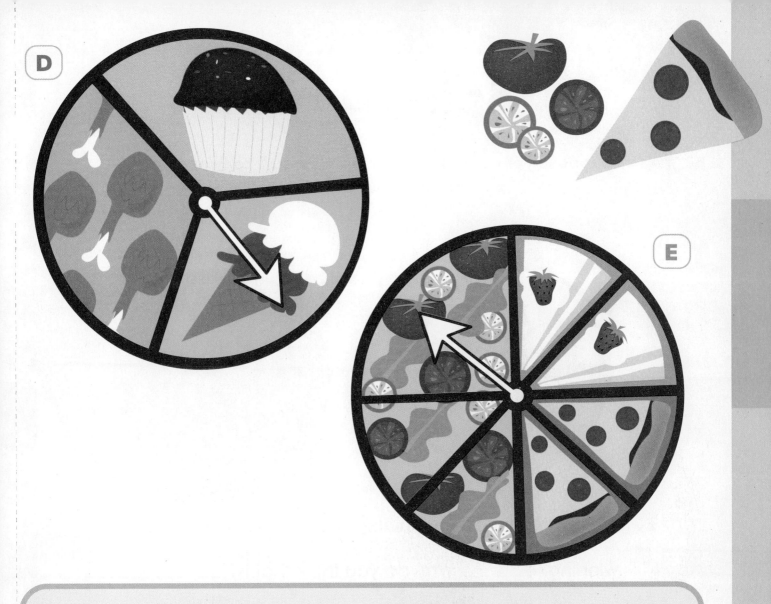

1. Which spinners show fair games, in which your chances of spinning any of the choices given are the same? _____

2. With which spinner do you have the best chance of spinning a dessert? _____

3. With which spinner do you have the best chance of spinning vegetables? _____

4. With which spinner do you have the best chance of spinning a main course? _____

Spin to Win!

Suppose your goal is to get from"Start" to "You Win!"
before your partner.

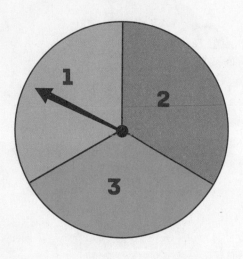 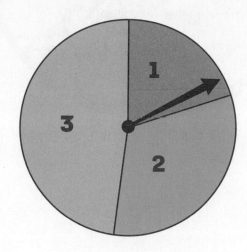

1. Which spinner do you think gives you the better chance of

winning? _____ Why do you think that is? _____

_____

2. If both players used the second spinner, would the game be

fair? _____ Why or why not? _____

_____

3. What else could you do to make this a fair game?

_____

You Win!

Organizing Data Answer Key

202–203 A. 15, 18, 21, 24 (count up by 3's), B. 21, 28, 36, 45 (add 2, then 3, then 4 and so on), C. 50, 45, 40, 35 (count down by 5's), D. 99, 12, 99, 13 (count up by 1, alternating with 99's), E. 64, 128, 256, 512 (multiply the previous number by 2), F. 11, 6, 13, 7 (alternating counting up by 1 with counting up by 2); each shape has one more side than the one before it, the next one should be seven sided.

204–205 rectangle, rectangle, square; 4 stacked boxes; shaded: bottom left box, bottom right box, top left box, 1 orange car, 1 purple car, 2 orange cars, 5 baby chicks, 1 hen; 42, 56, 72; $\frac{6}{12}, \frac{7}{14}, \frac{8}{16}$; 36, 49, 64, 1 minute and 48 seconds

206–207 10 (1 + 2 + 3 + 4), 16 (4 x 4); **triangular:** 3, 6, 10, 15, 21, 28, 36; **square:** 4, 9, 16, 25, 36; 36

208–209 **Circle** e, o, o, c, k, i, s; **slash** m, p, c, h, i; **put an X through** o, t, e, c, h, c, o, l, a; chocolate chimp cookies

210–211 Answers will vary.

212–213 **See below;** answers will vary.

214–215 **See below;** 1. lizards, 2. frogs, 3. robin red breasts, frogs, 4. alligators, tadpoles, 5. 29

216–217 1. 10,000,000 people, 2. cycling, 3. about 60,000,000, 4. about 10,000,000, 5. draw $2\frac{1}{2}$ sneakers; answers will vary

218–219 1. 15¢, 2. 22¢, 3. 7¢, 4. 1981, 5. 1991, 6. a. 45¢, b. $2.05

220–221 1. A and C, 2. D, 3. E, 4. B

222 1. spinner on the right; you have a greater chance of getting a 3; 2. yes; 3. answers will vary.

212–213

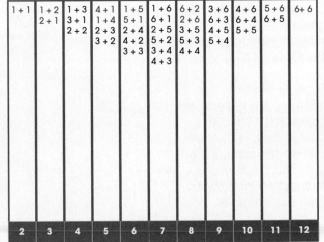

214–215

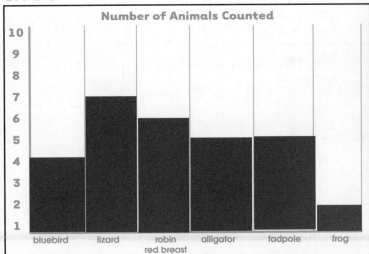

Math Skills

These essential math skill are covered in the following activity pages.